THE
BARBECUE

OVER 80 RECIPES TO IMPRESS AND INSPIRE!

ALEX HAMILTON

Harper
Collins

HarperCollins*Publishers*
1 London Bridge Street
London SE1 9GF

www.harpercollins.co.uk

First published by HarperCollins*Publishers* 2019

1 3 5 7 9 10 8 6 4 2

Recipes: Alex Hamilton & Jo Jackson
Photography: Charlotte Bland
Design, Art Direction & Prop Styling: Pene Parker Design
Food styling: Rukmini Iyer
Food stylist assistant: Jo Jackson

A catalogue record of this book is available from the British Library

ISBN 978-0-00-833397-3

Printed and bound in Latvia

MIX
Paper from
responsible sources
FSC™ C007454

This book is produced from independently certified FSC™ paper
to ensure responsible forest management.
For more information visit: www.harpercollins.co.uk/green

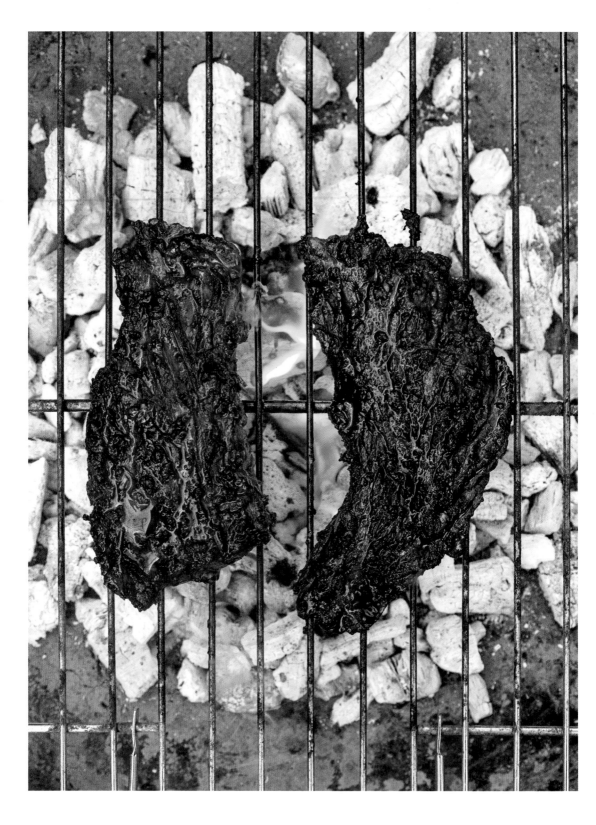

HOW TO USE THIS BOOK

This book is designed to be as user-friendly as possible, based on the idea that if you can get comfortable with one method for cooking something, then there's an infinite variety of ways to make it different and exciting the next time you do it. So, instead of giving you six different chicken recipes, in this book you get just one simple template for the 'hero' recipe, followed by a series of marinades you can pick from as you wish. The same goes for ribs, steak and vegetables, which are just glorious on a barbecue alongside punchy dressings and interesting salsas and salads.

We kick off with 'Things on Sticks' instead of a starter section, because they're a colourful, easy dish to prepare ahead, marinate, and stick on the barbecue as soon as your guests arrive. The main chapters (Ribs, Chicken, Whole Veg, Fish, Burgers, Steaks & Slow Cooking) are traditionally the stars of the show, and you can mix and match these, along with the tasty salsas and salads, depending on the occasion and how many you're feeding! If you're still hungry after the main event, the dessert section has some very easy but delicious recipes for barbecued fruit and indulgent s'mores.

Whether you're barbecuing in your back garden, or packing bits and pieces into a coolbox to take to the beach or park, this book has mix and match options that should keep you going all summer, and well into the autumn too. Head to page 154 for menu plan ideas to curate the perfect barbecue party table, with something to suit everyone. For tips on gas vs. charcoal and essential kit, see overleaf.

GAS VS CHARCOAL

CHARCOAL

Purists prefer charcoal for the smoky flavour, and I personally love that you can chuck rosemary, thyme, bay, sage or oregano on to the coals for a wonderful herbal scent as you cook. A kettle or lidded barbecue is really helpful for cooking your food evenly – if you're just using a very simple open grill or disposable barbecue, a really large inverted metal bowl will do at a pinch.

You will need: firelighters and long matches, or a long-handled lighter, as well as the charcoal. Set a couple of firelighters or plenty of scrunched-up paper under the coal, light them, then let the coal burn (20–25 minutes for lumpwood, up to 40 for briquettes) until they're evenly glowing and chalky grey – then you're good to start putting the food on.

Quick-cook items can be done over the coals (like things on sticks or steak). If you're cooking items for longer, like a whole chicken or thighs and drumsticks, you'll want to carefully move the coals to one side, and cook over the indirect heat on the other side of the barbecue.

Bear in mind, if you're barbecuing for a long time, you will want to have another load of hot coals ready to tip onto the barbecue for when your first lot has died down – this is easy to get going in an inexpensive chimney starter.

GAS

For ease and convenience, gas is incredibly helpful. You certainly get a slightly different, less smoky finish on your food, but with the lid down the barbecue will heat up in under 10 minutes, and you can regulate the intensity of the flame just by turning the dial – very hassle-free. You may find, depending on your model, that there are hot and cold spots, so, using something fairly inexpensive like grilled vegetables, do a little test moving your food around to see where the hot and cool spots are.

ESSENTIAL KIT

Other than a barbecue, there's very little kit that you need, so I'd start with:

TONGS: Now, a key consideration with barbecuing is cross-contamination. If you put your raw chicken on the barbecue with your tongs, flip it over halfway, then take it off, all with the same tongs without washing in between, you've just potentially contaminated the cooked chicken with salmonella. Get two sets of long-handled tongs, one for raw meat and one for cooked, and don't confuse them.

FLIPPER: A long-handled flipper is helpful for burgers – again, you should use two: one for raw and one for cooked meat.

TRAYS: The same goes with trays or dishes – use one to take your raw, marinated food out to the barbecue, and once it's cooked, transfer the food on to a clean, fresh tray or plate.

OTHER: You do tend to get other bits of kit in a barbecue set – long-handled forks and such, but I tend to stick to the tongs and the flipper, as they'll pick up and turn most things. A very stiff wire brush is helpful for cleaning the grill.

Note on the recipes: When the recipe instructs you to add the meat, fish or veg to the barbecue, your barbecue should already be hot and ready to cook on, whether using gas or coals – see page 9.

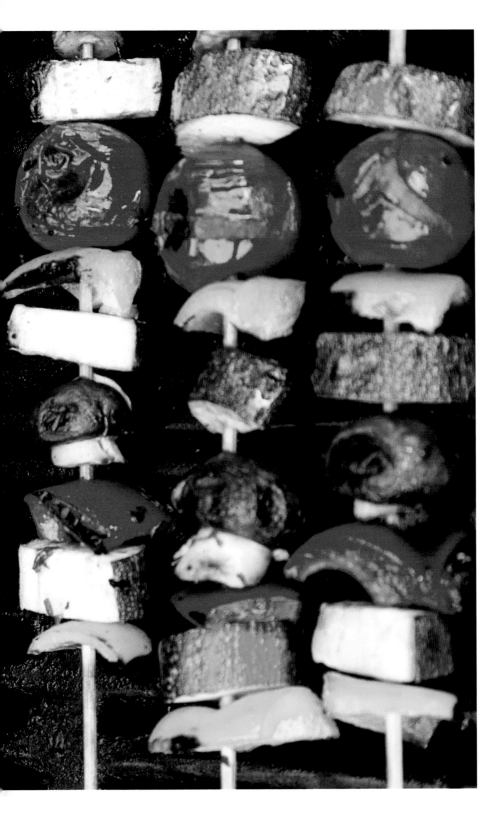

I love food on sticks – it's both a practical and a decorative way to cook a variety of meat, vegetables or fish quickly, and a great way to kick off a barbecue, as you'll have prepared everything in advance. There's good culinary precedent for it – it makes me think of eating proper satay at the roadside in Asia, where incredibly delicious marinated meat skewers are barbecued on open grills. It's easy to make vegetarian or vegan versions – try the options below for paneer, halloumi or tofu with a variety of vegetables.

This chapter includes suggestions for things you can put on sticks, the quantities you might need, and, in the pages that follow, the simple marinades that you can use for any of the below.

A note on skewers: the metal ones are really the best, as they will heat up and help to cook your food from the inside. If using bamboo or wooden ones, soak them in water for 30 minutes or so before you start cooking.

BEEF, PORK, LAMB & CHORIZO

With beef, pork or lamb, you want cuts that will stay tender when cooked quickly.

WHAT TYPE?

BEEF: rump steak, or sirloin if you're splashing out.

PORK: go for tenderloin, pork steaks or chops.

LAMB: try lamb rump or lamb steaks.

CHORIZO: use mini cooking chorizo sausages, or cut 1cm rounds from a larger chorizo sausage.

With beef, pork or lamb, you can cut the meat into roughly 2.5cm cubes, but I prefer to cut the meat into long strips, about 1.5cm wide and deep, then thread the strips back and forward on to skewers in an S shape, push them down, and continue – that way you get the maximum surface area to nicely char on the barbecue, and only have to flip the skewer on two sides rather than four.

HOW MUCH?

Allow about 100g of meat per person as a starter. You can intersperse vegetables from the veg section and chorizo along with the meat if you wish, or make them up as separate skewers.

Pick a marinade from the suggestions on the following pages, make it up in a large shallow bowl (rectangular glass Pyrex dishes are good for this), then stir through the strips of meat.

Thread the meat on to the skewers, then cover and leave to marinate in the fridge for a couple of hours to overnight.

Barbecue

Once your barbecue is good and hot (see page 9), lay the skewers on the grill and cook for 6–7 minutes, covered if your barbecue can be covered. Turn the skewers over and give them another 6–7 minutes or so. The meat should be well charred on the outside, and a thermometer inserted into the thickest part of the flesh (don't hit the metal skewer, or the reading will be off) should show at least 70°C.

Let them rest on a plate for 3–4 minutes, then serve with your choice of dipping sauce (see pages 32–41).

SALMON

WHAT TYPE?

Use big salmon fillets that you can cut into even, 4cm chunks. (You need to have decent-sized chunks, as the fish is very quick to cook.)

HOW MUCH?

Allow 100–120g of salmon per person as a generous starter. You can make up the salmon skewers by themselves, or pick a variety of vegetables to flesh them out – I like to use red and yellow peppers or cherry tomatoes for colour.

Pick a marinade from the suggestions on the following pages, omitting any lime or lemon juice, as this will 'cook' the salmon too early.

Thread the salmon and any vegetables on to the skewers, then cover and leave to marinate in the fridge for a couple of hours to overnight.

Barbecue

Once your barbecue is good and hot (see page 9), gently brush the grill with olive oil. This is important, as the fish will want to stick. Lay the salmon skewers on the grill and cook for 5 minutes, covered if your barbecue can be covered. Turn the skewers over and give them another 4–5 minutes or so. The fish should be well charred on the outside, and a thermometer inserted into the flesh (don't hit the metal skewer, or the reading will be off) should show at least 65°C.

Serve immediately, with your choice of dipping sauce (see pages 32–41).

PRAWNS

WHAT TYPE?

Ideally, use whole, shell-on prawns, or my favourite, the headless type with half a shell and a tail on, readily available in supermarkets; the shell will protect the delicate flesh from the heat of the barbecue. You can also use shelled prawns, but they'll cook much quicker.

HOW MUCH?

Allow 80–90g of prawns per person as a starter (a bit more if they're fully shell-on with heads, etc.). You can make up the prawn skewers by themselves, or add in your choice of vegetables from the vegetable section overleaf.

Pick a marinade from the suggestions on the following pages, omitting any lime or lemon juice, as this will 'cook' the prawns too early. If you're going to make my favourite pepper, salt and lime prawns, don't marinate them before cooking – just toss the raw prawns with a little olive oil.

Thread the prawns on to the skewers, then cover and leave to marinate in the fridge for a couple of hours to overnight. (Unless you're just doing them with olive oil, in which case you're ready to cook straight away.)

Barbecue

Once your barbecue is good and hot (see page 9), gently lay the prawn skewers on the grill and cook for 2–3 minutes, covered if your barbecue can be covered. Turn the skewers over, using a pair of tongs, and give them another 2–3 minutes. They are ready when they're bright pink on the outside, and the shells should be a little charred.

Serve immediately, with your choice of dipping sauce (see pages 32–41).

VEGETABLES

Marinated vegetables work beautifully on skewers. Use the combination below, or add halloumi, paneer or tofu. I like a good mixture of colours and texture on skewers, and would usually go for the following:

WHAT TYPE?

150g whole baby chestnut mushrooms

200g baby courgettes, cut into 1.5cm squares

1 red pepper, cut into 1.5cm squares

1 yellow pepper, cut into 1.5cm squares

300g whole cherry tomatoes

1 red onion, cut into small wedges

1 aubergine, cut into 1.5cm cubes

HOW MUCH?

The quantity of vegetables above will make up at least 15–20 skewers without any further additions, so they're a generous veggie starter for a crowd.

Pick a marinade from the suggestions on the following pages, make it up in a large shallow bowl (rectangular glass Pyrex dishes are good for this), then stir through the vegetables.

Thread the veg on to the skewers, then cover and leave to marinate in the fridge for a couple of hours to overnight.

Barbecue

Once your barbecue is good and hot (see page 9), lay the skewers on the grill and cook for about 6–7 minutes, covered if your barbecue can be covered. Turn the skewers over and give them another 6–7 minutes or so. The vegetables should be cooked through, and nicely charred in places – flip them and give them another 3–4 minutes if in doubt.

Serve immediately, with your choice of dip (see pages 32–41).

HALLOUMI, PANEER & TOFU

Halloumi, paneer and tofu all barbecue really well, and a good marinade will add flavour and texture from the interesting charred bits.

WHAT TYPE?

HALLOUMI: pick the nicest one you can, as it makes a real difference to the flavour and texture.

PANEER: you can buy this packaged in blocks (a bit like feta cheese) in many supermarkets – it works beautifully on the barbecue.

TOFU: you definitely want a block of firm tofu for this (silken will fall apart). My favourite brand is Tofoo – the smoked one is particularly good.

Cut your halloumi, paneer or tofu chunks into 2.5cm cubes – not too small, or they'll be difficult to skewer.

HOW MUCH?

Allow about 80–100g of halloumi, paneer or tofu per person as a starter. You can intersperse vegetables from the veg section as well if you wish, or make them up as separate skewers.

Pick a marinade from the suggestions on the following pages, make it up in a large shallow bowl (rectangular glass Pyrex dishes are good for this), then stir through the paneer, tofu or halloumi cubes.

Thread the cubes on to the skewers, then cover and leave to marinate in the fridge for a couple of hours to overnight.

Barbecue

Once your barbecue is good and hot (see page 9), lay the skewers on the grill and cook for about 5 minutes, covered if your barbecue can be covered. Turn the skewers over and give them another 5 minutes or so, then turn them on to their sides to char for another 3–4 minutes. The cheese or tofu should be evenly charred on the outside.

Serve immediately, with your choice of dipping sauce (see pages 32–41).

CHICKEN

Chicken breast is a good option for skewers, as they'll cook quickly and any of the marinades you pick will help tenderise the chicken.

WHAT TYPE?

Cut chicken breasts into 2.5cm chunks – or I quite like to use packets of mini fillets, as you can weave them on to the skewers without any further chopping.

HOW MUCH?

Allow about 100g of chicken per person as a starter. I prefer to make up chicken skewers by themselves, and serve vegetable skewers separately on the side.

Pick a marinade from the suggestions on the following pages, make it up in a large shallow bowl (rectangular glass Pyrex dishes are good for this), then stir through the chicken pieces.

Thread the chicken on to the skewers, then cover and leave to marinate in the fridge for a couple of hours to overnight.

Barbecue

Once your barbecue is good and hot (see page 9), lay the chicken skewers on the grill and cook for 6–7 minutes, covered if your barbecue can be covered. Turn the skewers over and give them another 6–7 minutes or so. The chicken should be well charred on the outside, and a thermometer inserted into the thickest part of the flesh (don't hit the metal skewer, or the reading will be off) should show at least 70°C.

Serve immediately, with your choice of dipping sauce (see pages 32–41).

PEPPERCORN, SALT & LIME

I first had this barbecue dressing in Vietnam, where they served freshly grilled prawns in the shell with a dipping bowl of this incredible mixture alongside; I give you my version below. It's very simple and very effective – do use really good, freshly ground black peppercorns, or try a variation with Sichuan peppercorns. This will make enough for about 400g of meat, fish or veg.

2 tbsp black peppercorns

1½ tsp sea salt flakes

1 lime, juice only
(make sure it's a juicy lime)

1 tbsp olive oil

WORKS WELL WITH

Prawns (see page 18)
Halloumi (see page 22)
Chicken (see page 24)
Salmon (see page 17)
Beef (see page 16)
Tofu (see page 22)
Paneer (see page 22)

Use your pepper grinder or a pestle and mortar to coarsely grind the black peppercorns – I know it's time-consuming, but this is the essence of the marinade. (Under no circumstances use ready-ground black pepper – it will make your dish taste of dust.)

Stir the freshly ground pepper with the sea salt, lime juice and olive oil. Now, if you're using this as a dipping sauce for grilled prawns or fish, pop most of it into a few little bowls, and once your prawns/fish cubes are barbecued (see pages 18 and 17), tip them into the mixing bowl with the remaining black pepper dressing. Give them a quick toss, then serve immediately with the little bowls of extra dressing and plenty of paper towels for people to discard their prawn shells and clean up.

If you're using this as a pre-cooking marinade, dunk your meat or vegetables into the marinade, then cover, refrigerate and leave to marinate for a couple of hours to overnight before barbecuing.

LEMON, OREGANO & GARLIC

I love the Mediterranean flavours in this simple, effective marinade. This will make enough for at least 750g of whatever you want to barbecue. Do note, if you're going to use it for fish or prawns, omit the lemon juice and squeeze it over at the end instead – the fish will 'cook' if left to marinate in the acid.

1 lemon, zest and juice

20g fresh oregano, leaves finely chopped

3 tbsp olive oil

Freshly ground black pepper

2 garlic cloves, finely grated

2 tsp sea salt flakes

Mix all the ingredients together in a large bowl. Tip your prepared meat, fish, veg or a mixture into the marinade, mix well, then cover and refrigerate for a couple of hours to overnight until you're ready to barbecue.

WORKS WELL WITH

Chicken (see page 24)
Beef (see page 16)
Pork (see page 16)
Lamb (see page 16)
Paneer (see page 22)
Tofu (see page 22)

TANDOORI SPICES & YOGURT

Probably my favourite marinade, but then I'm biased because the smell of tandoori spices on a barbecue just makes me think of summer. This recipe will make enough for at least 750g of whatever you want to barbecue. Do note, if you're going to use it for fish or prawns, omit the lemon juice and squeeze it over at the end instead – the fish will 'cook' if left to marinate in the acid.

6 tbsp natural yogurt

1 tbsp olive oil

1 large lemon, zest and juice

5 garlic cloves, grated

5cm ginger, peeled and grated

2 heaped tsp ground cumin

1 tsp ground turmeric

2 heaped tsp smoked paprika

1 tsp mild chilli powder

A good grind of freshly ground black pepper

1½ tsp sea salt flakes

Mix all the ingredients together in a large bowl. Tip your prepared meat, fish, veg or a mixture into the marinade, mix well, then cover and refrigerate for a couple of hours to overnight until you're ready to barbecue.

WORKS WELL WITH

Salmon (see page 17)

Chicken (see page 24)

Beef (see page 16)

Chorizo (see page 16)

Vegetables (see page 20)

Halloumi (see page 22)

Paneer (see page 22)

ROSEMARY, CAYENNE & BROWN SUGAR

This rich, sticky, sweet and spicy marinade with rosemary will make your garden smell incredible. For an even more intense rosemary hit, after you've stripped the rosemary sprigs of needles, use them as mini skewers for whatever you're barbecuing. This recipe will make enough for at least 750g of whatever you want to barbecue. Do note, if you're going to use it for fish or prawns, omit the lime juice and squeeze it over at the end instead – the fish will 'cook' if left to marinate in the acid.

20g fresh rosemary sprigs

1 lime, zest and juice

1 tsp cayenne pepper

2 tsp sea salt flakes

3 tbsp olive oil

2 heaped tbsp dark brown sugar

Strip the needles off the rosemary sprigs, then finely chop them and mix with the other ingredients in a large bowl. Tip your prepared meat, fish, veg or a mixture into the marinade, mix well, then cover and refrigerate for a couple of hours to overnight until you're ready to barbecue.

If you're going to use some of the rosemary sprigs as skewers, use something sharp to pierce the food first before threading it on to the rosemary.

WORKS WELL WITH

Chicken (see page 24)
Beef (see page 16)
Pork (see page 16)
Lamb (see page 16)
Paneer (see page 22)
Tofu (see page 22)

PERFECT GUACAMOLE

LIME & CORIANDER
TZATZIKI

MEXICAN CHILLI
PEANUT SAUCE

SIMPLE SOUR CREAM
& SPRING ONION DIP

SAFFRON MAYONNAISE

HOT SATAY SAUCE

MEXICAN CHILLI PEANUT SAUCE

This spicy chilli peanut sauce is so addictive that you will want to put it on everything – I've been known to have it in a cheese sandwich. You will need chiles de árbol for this recipe, which are very easy to find online – it's worth getting them to be able to whip up a batch of this sauce.

Makes: 1 jar, to keep in the fridge

2 tbsp olive oil

4 chiles de árbol, deseeded

1 garlic clove, peeled

150g unsalted blanched peanuts

Sea salt flakes

Heat the olive oil in a large frying pan and add the chiles de árbol, garlic and peanuts. Fry them over a medium-low heat, stirring frequently, for about 10 minutes, until all the peanuts are an even golden brown.

Tip everything on to a plate and leave to cool down for about 15 minutes.

Transfer everything to a blender or food processor, along with a teaspoon of sea salt and 150ml of water. Blitz until smooth, adding more water a tablespoon at a time until you have a sauce about the consistency of double cream. Taste, adjust the salt, and keep in a jar in the fridge for up to a week.

WORKS WELL WITH

Any Peppercorn, Salt & Lime flavoured
  skewers (see page 26)
Classic or Sticky Hot Chipotle Ribs
  (see pages 49 and 50)
Pollo al Carbón (see page 64)
Whole veg with Chilli, Lime & Coriander
  Dressing (see page 82)
Grilled Fish Tacos (see page 90)
Barbecue Brisket (see page 120)

HOT SATAY SAUCE

Sambal oelek is an Indonesian chilli paste made primarily from crushed chillies and vinegar. Sambal refers to the chilli sauce, while oelek, a word of Dutch origin, refers to a stoneware dish, similar to a pestle and mortar, which is used to crush spices in Indonesian kitchens.

Makes: about 300ml, enough for 4

4 garlic cloves

4 shallots, peeled, roots removed
   and halved

2 tbsp sambal oelek paste

2 tbsp vegetable oil

A pinch of chilli flakes

200g peanuts, toasted and lightly crushed

200ml coconut milk

100ml water

1 tbsp brown sugar

1/2 lime, juice only

Sea salt flakes

Place the garlic, shallots and sambal oelek in a food processor and blitz until a smooth paste is formed.

Heat a heavy-based pan and add the oil. Once the oil is sizzling, empty the contents of the food processor into the pan along with the chilli flakes. Turn the temperature down and cook over a low heat for 20–30 minutes. You are looking for an obvious change in the colour of the paste – it will go from a bright to a more muted, terracotta red.

Next, add the peanuts to the pan along with the coconut milk and water. Mix together and simmer gently for a further 5 minutes. If you think it looks a little thick, add some more coconut milk and water. After 5 minutes, remove from the heat and add the sugar, lime juice and a generous pinch of sea salt. Serve immediately, or keep in a sterilised jar in the fridge for up to a week.

WORKS WELL WITH

Chicken skewers (see page 24)
Beef, pork or lamb skewers (see page 16)
Salmon skewers (see page 17)
Whole Aubergine (see page 69)

CORIANDER & LIME TZATZIKI

This is so refreshing, and works as a dip with almost anything (I've been known to dunk pieces of baguette in before now).

Makes: enough for 4

1 cucumber

300ml Greek yogurt

½ garlic clove, crushed

30g fresh coriander, finely chopped

1 lime, zest and juice

1 tsp olive oil

Sea salt flakes

Halve, deseed and grate the cucumber. Sprinkle with a generous pinch of sea salt and let it sit in a colander for 20 minutes or so.

After 20 minutes, give the cucumber a good squeeze and drain away its juices. Combine with the remaining ingredients in a bowl. Taste and adjust the seasoning if necessary. The flavour of the tzatziki will benefit from being made ahead of time; either serve straight away, or prep ahead and keep in the fridge until you need it.

WORKS WELL WITH

Any snack or appetisers of your choice
Vegetable skewers (see page 20)
Chicken skewers (see page 24)

SIMPLE SOUR CREAM & SPRING ONION DIP

Makes: enough for 4

227ml sour cream

1 small bunch of spring onions, finely chopped

1 lime, zest and juice

Sea salt flakes

Combine all the ingredients in a bowl and mix well. Taste and check the seasoning and acidity – you are looking for a nice zesty flavour. Serve immediately, or keep in the fridge until needed.

WORKS WELL WITH

Smoked Paprika and Lemon Chicken (see page 62)
Whole Portobello Mushrooms & Asparagus (see page 68)
Smoky Black Bean Burgers (see page 104)
Sticky Hot Chipotle Ribs (see page 50)

PERFECT GUACAMOLE

Perfect guacamole is a big claim – but out of all the variations that I've tried, this has to be my favourite. The not so secret way to make it perfect? Taste, adjust, taste and adjust again – the right combination of lime juice and salt will make this guac sing.

Makes: 1 large bowl

4 ripe avocados

1 small red onion, very finely chopped

2 small tomatoes, finely chopped

30g fresh coriander, finely chopped

2–3 limes, juice only

2 tsp sea salt flakes

Roughly chop or mash the avocado flesh (depending whether you like smooth-ish or chopped guac), then stir through the onion, tomatoes and coriander.

Now, add most of the lime juice and salt, and taste. Does it need more of both? Keep adding a hefty squeeze of lime juice and pinches of sea salt flakes, tasting as you go, until it tastes just right to you.

Make ahead: With the industrial amounts of lime juice, this guac will be fine made a couple of hours ahead and fridged – just press some clingfilm over the top to prevent it oxidising.

Mix it up suggestions: Add crispy bacon, crumbled Roquefort or black beans.

WORKS WELL WITH

Tortilla chips or Grilled Fish Tacos
   (see page 90)
Classic Beef Burgers (see page 98)
Chickpea & Carrot Burgers
   (see page 105)
Smoky Black Bean Burgers (see page 104)
Barbecue Brisket (see page 120)

SPRUCE UP YOUR MAYO

Once you have basic homemade mayonnaise down, either by hand or in a food processor, there are so many ways you can flavour it – I've suggested three below.

Makes: about 175ml, enough for 4

Basic mayonnaise 1

1 egg yolk

175ml neutral-tasting oil

Sea salt flakes

Freshly ground black pepper

Basic mayonnaise 2

1 egg yolk

175ml neutral-tasting oil

Sea salt flakes

Freshly ground black pepper

1 tsp Dijon mustard

1 tbsp lemon juice

Chipotle Mayonnaise

1–2 tbsp chipotle paste

Garlic Mayonnaise

½ garlic clove, crushed

Saffron Mayonnaise

A pinch of saffron strands, infused
  in 1 tbsp boiling water for 10 minutes

Basic mayonnaise 1: Place the egg yolk in a deep bowl and whisk gently to break it up a little. Using a bottle with a nozzle, drip in the oil one drop at a time; or in a very slow, steady stream. Once you've added half of the oil you can add it a little faster. But continue to do so slowly. Once all of the oil has been added, you can let it down with a teaspoon of water if it looks too thick. Season generously and taste.

Basic mayonnaise 2: Place the egg yolk, mustard, lemon juice, salt and pepper in the small bowl of a food processor. Blitz briefly. Next, with the mixer running, drip in the oil one drop at a time; or in a very slow, steady stream. Once you've added half of the oil you can add it a little faster. But continue to do so slowly. Once all of the oil has been added, you can let it down with a teaspoon of water if it looks too thick. Season generously and taste.

Once you are happy with your basic mayonnaise you can spruce it up with any of the flavourings suggested opposite. Simply stir into your mayonnaise. Cover and chill until ready to serve. The mayonnaise will keep in the fridge for up to 3 days.

ULTIMATE CHILLI OIL

I first saw a friend of mine make this, slightly terrifyingly, with the boiling oil poured directly over a little pot of chilli flakes. This version reverses her method for a delicious, and somewhat less hazardous condiment . . .

Makes: 1 small jar

75ml vegetable or olive oil

40g crushed chilli flakes (around this amount is fine, whatever your standard supermarket size is)

WORKS WELL WITH

Beef, pork, halloumi, paneer or veg skewers
   (see pages 16, 22 and 20)
Whole Aubergine or Long-stem Broccoli
   (see pages 69 and 79)
Salmon or whole trout
   (see pages 17 and 92)
Pork, Fennel & Apple Burgers
   (see page 100)
Chickpea & Carrot Burgers
   (see page 105)
Smoky Black Bean Burgers (see page 104)
Barbecue Brisket (see page 120)

Put the oil into a small, deep saucepan and heat it through over a low heat for 5 minutes. If you cautiously wave your hand over the top of the pan, it should feel warm, but the oil shouldn't be smoking.

Turn off the heat, then open a window and put your extractor fan on. This is important, because now you're going to tip the chilli flakes into the hot oil, and they can give off pretty strong chilli fumes. Once the chilli flakes are in, give the pan a gentle swirl so they're all submerged in the oil – they'll be bubbling like a witch's cauldron at this point. Pop a lid on the pan, and leave the oil to completely cool down before pouring it into a small lidded jar or bottle. This will keep for a couple of months.

SWEET HABANERO SAUCE

Although originally from Brazil, habanero chillies are widely grown and used in Mexican cooking. They rate pretty highly on the spice scale, but used sparingly, they make an excellent accompaniment to any barbecued meat. I'd go as far as to say they make an excellent accompaniment to literally anything on the barbecue if you like spice. The dark brown sugar in this recipe brings a wonderful, sweet caramel flavour to complement the heat of the chilli.

Makes: enough for 6, generously

20g dried habanero chillies

100ml boiling water

1 red onion, roughly chopped

½ tsp sea salt flakes

2 tbsp olive oil

1 garlic clove

3–4 tbsp dark brown sugar

Put the chillies into a bowl, cover with the boiling water and let them rehydrate for about 30 minutes. Remove the chillies from the bowl but reserve the water. (I'd recommend using rubber gloves for the next step!) Remove the stalks and deseed the chillies. If you're feeling particularly daring, you might like to leave the seeds in.

Place the chillies in a food processor with the red onion, salt, olive oil and garlic. Blitz until a smooth paste is formed, adding 2 tablespoons of the chilli water to loosen if required. Heat a small saucepan and empty the contents of the food processor into it. Add the sugar, bring to a gentle boil and simmer for about 5 minutes. If the sauce looks too thick, loosen with a little more of the chilli water.

Taste to check the sweetness and seasoning. Allow to cool before serving, or transfer to a sterilised jar and keep in the fridge for up to a week.

WORKS WELL WITH

Grilled Fish Tacos (see page 90)
Pork Pibil (see page 116)

FIERY SCOTCH BONNET SAUCE

Chilli, onion and garlic are a match made in heaven. This fiery sauce celebrates their union. Use it to complement some chargrilled broccoli or cauliflower.

Makes: 1 small jar

---

1 red onion, roughly chopped

3 garlic cloves, peeled

6 Scotch bonnet chillies, deseeded and stalks removed

3 tbsp olive oil

6 tbsp water

Sea salt flakes

Place all the ingredients in a food processor, along with a pinch of salt, and blitz until smooth. Heat a small saucepan and put the contents of the food processor into it. Bring to the boil, then simmer for 5 minutes. Add more water to loosen the sauce if necessary.

WORKS WELL WITH

Classic Beef Burgers (see page 98)
Chickpea & Carrot Burgers (see page 105)
Smoky Black Bean Burgers (see page 104)

PINK PICKLED ONIONS

This is one of the quickest pickles you can make – it not only looks beautiful, but works beautifully with everything from burgers to slow-cooked pork.

Makes: 1 small bowl

1 large red onion, very thinly sliced

1–2 juicy limes

A pinch of sea salt flakes

Tip the sliced onion into a small pan of boiling water and let it cook for 30 seconds. Drain the onion really well in a colander.

Put the drained onions into a bowl and stir through the lime juice (if your lime isn't very juicy, use two), along with a big pinch of sea salt. Let the onions sit for 30 minutes to an hour, stirring occasionally, and watch as they turn a luminous pink. Taste and add more sea salt as needed, and either serve immediately or keep in a jar in the fridge for 2–3 days.

WORKS WELL WITH

Smoked Paprika & Lemon Chicken
  (see page 62)
Classic Beef Burgers (see page 98)
Smoky Black Bean Burgers (see page 104)
Pork Pibil (see page 116)
Grilled Fish Tacos (see page 90)

DILL PICKLES

If you're in a hurry, you can make the quick version of these pickles below in version 2, but for a jar to dip into during the week, the first is a lovely storecupboard standby to go with burgers.

Makes: enough to fill a 500ml Kilner jar

250ml cider vinegar

250ml water

150g caster sugar

1 tsp dill seeds, lightly crushed

1 tsp coriander seeds, lightly crushed

1 tsp fine salt

6 black peppercorns

¼ cucumber, sliced into batons lengthways, and/or 250g baby aubergines, sliced lengthways

Version 1: Place the vinegar, water, sugar, dill seeds, coriander seeds, salt and peppercorns into a small saucepan, bring to a gentle boil, then simmer for 2 minutes. Allow to cool.

Put the vegetables into a sterilised jar and pour over the pickling solution. Leave overnight before serving.

The pickles will keep in an airtight jar or container for up to a week.

Version 2: Using a mandolin, cut the cucumber into thin slices.

Place the vinegar, water, sugar, dill seeds, coriander seeds, salt and peppercorns into a small saucepan, bring to a gentle boil, then simmer for 2 minutes. Allow to cool.

Put the cucumber into a sterilised jar and pour over the pickling solution. Leave for about an hour before serving.

WORKS WELL WITH

Classic Beef Burgers (see page 98)
Spicy Lamb Kofte Burgers (see page 102)

QUICK KIMCHI

I'm not sure when I started actively craving kimchi at dinnertime, but when it's this quick to make, that's no bad thing. You can make this version with an ordinary white supermarket cabbage, and while it's ready to eat as soon as you make it, it'll taste even nicer fermented after a couple of days.

Makes: a 1 litre jar

1kg white cabbage

30g sea salt flakes

250ml water

40g Korean red pepper flakes (gochugaru)

6 garlic cloves, very finely chopped

1 small carrot, grated

4 spring onions, thinly sliced

70ml fish sauce (or use soy sauce
   if vegetarian)

WORKS WELL WITH

Ribs with Korean Barbecue Marinade
   (see pages 48 and 61)
Whole veg with Chilli, Lime & Coriander
   Dressing (see page 82)
Classic Beef Burgers (see page 98)
Smoky Black Bean Burgers (see page 104)

Quarter the cabbage, then slice it very finely into strips, discarding any really tough bits. Pop the sea salt flakes into a large bowl, add a splash of boiling water to dissolve them, then top it up with the remaining water. Add the sliced cabbage, and work it into the salted water really well with your hands. Leave to salt for 15 minutes, stirring once.

Meanwhile, prepare all your other ingredients and mix together in a large bowl. Once the cabbage has had 15 minutes, drain it really well, then rinse it in a couple of changes of cold water before squeezing it dry with a tea towel. Stir it through your red pepper mixture. The kimchi is ready to eat now.

Make ahead: For fermented kimchi, you can make this anything from a few days to a month ahead. Press the kimchi into a jar or glass container into which it'll all fit snugly, then use the back of a spoon to press it down to eliminate air pockets. Pop the lid on, then leave it to ferment at room temperature for a couple of days, pressing the cabbage down into the liquid each day. After 2–3 days, store in the fridge for up to a month.

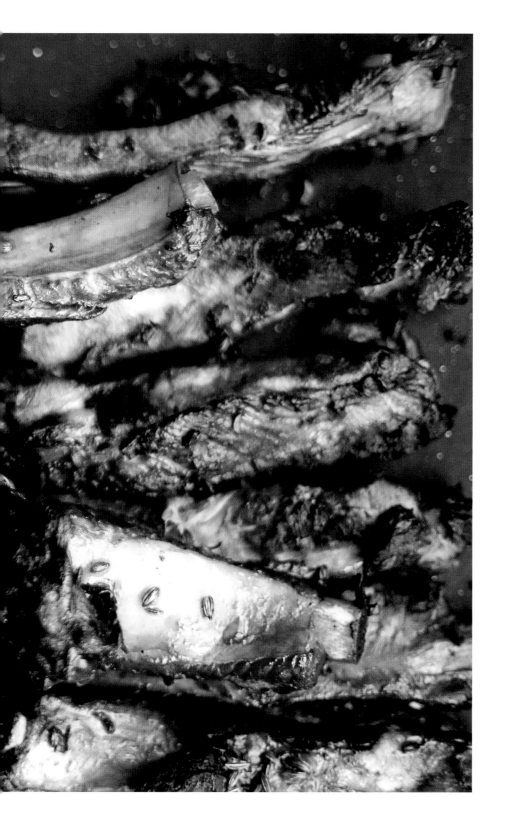

RIBS

One method. Three unique flavours. These ribs are an excellent way to demonstrate how you can use the same cooking method but a different flavour map of ingredients to create marinades from three distinct corners of the world.

Makes: enough for 4

---

2 x 500g baby racks of pork ribs, 1kg sliced short ribs or 2 beef short ribs per person

Your chosen marinade (see pages 49–52)

Rub the marinade into the ribs and leave for a few hours, or better still, overnight.

Preheat the oven to 160°C/140°C Fan/Gas 3.

Place the ribs and marinade in an oven dish and add a thin layer of water to the bottom of the dish to prevent the ribs from drying out during cooking.

Wrap the dish tightly in foil and cook in the oven for 4 hours, or until the ribs are just falling apart. Check once or twice during cooking to ensure they are not drying out.

Finish the ribs on the barbecue over a high heat, for 5 minutes or so, until they are charred on each side.

CLASSIC BARBECUE MARINADE

This is a classic barbecue marinade – people can get really technical about this, but what you want is a blend of sweet and salty, with a touch of spice. This will caramelise beautifully on the barbecue.

Makes: enough for 4

---

2 x 500g baby racks of pork ribs, 1kg sliced short ribs or 2 beef short ribs per person

For the marinade

1 tbsp olive oil

1 tbsp soy sauce

1 tbsp Worcestershire sauce

2 tbsp tomato purée

2 tbsp dark muscovado sugar

1 tbsp smooth Dijon mustard

½ tsp chilli powder (optional)

Mix together the olive oil, soy sauce, Worcestershire sauce, tomato purée, sugar, mustard and chilli powder (if using) in a shallow dish or roasting tin big enough to hold all the ribs in one layer. Add the ribs, turn to cover in the marinade, then cover and refrigerate for 2 hours to overnight.

See opposite for the oven + barbecue ribs cooking instructions.

WORKS WELL WITH

Simple Sour Cream & Spring Onion Dip
   (see page 35)
Pickled Watermelon Rind (see page 126)
Pineapple, Chilli & Mint Salsa
   (see page 127)
Classic Coleslaw (see page 130)
And for extra pigginess, Classic Potato
   Salad with bacon (see page 139)

STICKY HOT CHIPOTLE MARINADE

Makes: enough for 4

2 x 500g baby racks of pork ribs, 1kg sliced short ribs or 2 beef short ribs per person

For the marinade

2 tbsp vegetable oil

1 red onion, finely chopped

2 garlic cloves, crushed

50g dark brown sugar

1 tbsp chipotle paste

1 lemon, zest only

1 tbsp malt or white vinegar

2 sprigs of fresh rosemary, needles finely chopped

15g fresh tarragon, finely chopped

Fine sea salt

Heat a large frying pan. Pour in the oil and when it is hot add the onion. Add a pinch of salt and sauté over a medium heat for 5–10 minutes, until it has softened and taken on a little colour.

Once the onion has browned, add the garlic and fry for another couple of minutes. Next add the sugar, chipotle paste, lemon rind, vinegar, herbs and 100ml of water. Bring the sauce to the boil, then reduce the heat and simmer for 5 minutes or so, until the sauce has thickened.

Taste and check the seasoning.

Turn to page 48 for the oven + barbecue ribs cooking instructions.

WORKS WELL WITH

Pink Pickled Onions (see page 42)
Sour Cream and Spring Onion Dip
   (see page 35)
Pineapple, Chilli and Mint Salsa
   (see page 127)

JERK RIBS

You can buy jerk seasoning ready-made, but just a few spices that you probably already have in the cupboard will make you a jar of homemade, which you'll end up using through the season for jerk ribs and chicken.

Makes: enough for 4

2 x 500g baby racks of pork ribs, 1kg sliced short ribs or 2 beef short ribs per person

For the jerk paste

4 tbsp jerk seasoning (see right)

4 spring onions, roughly chopped

½ onion, roughly chopped

5 garlic cloves, peeled

5cm ginger, peeled

3 tbsp dark brown sugar

1 lime, juice only

2 heaped tsp sea salt flakes

2 Scotch bonnet chillies, deseeded

2 tbsp vegetable oil

WORKS WELL WITH

Simple Sour Cream & Spring Onion Dip
   (see page 35)
Pickled Watermelon Rind (see page 126)
Pineapple, Chilli & Mint Salsa
   (see page 127)
Classic Coleslaw (see page 130)
Classic Potato Salad (see page 139)

Blitz all the ingredients in a food processor or blender until you have a rough paste. Rub this all over the ribs, then cover and leave to marinate in the fridge for a couple of hours to overnight.

Turn to page 48 for the oven + barbecue ribs cooking instructions.

HOMEMADE JERK SEASONING

3 tbsp allspice berries

3 cinnamon sticks

5 tbsp black peppercorns

5 tbsp dried thyme

3 tsp cayenne pepper

3 tsp sea salt

¾ nutmeg, freshly grated

Toast the above together in a large, dry frying pan over a low heat for 10 minutes, stirring frequently, until it smells toasty.

Let it cool down completely, then blitz in a grinder or with a pestle and mortar. Keep in a lidded jar for a couple of months.

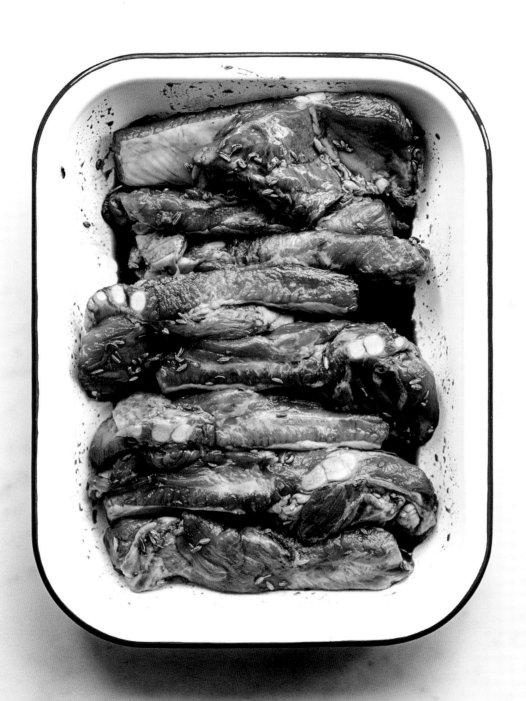

CHICKEN: THIGHS, DRUMSTICKS, SPATCHCOCKED

Save the chicken breast for skewers – the best type of chicken to cook from scratch is chicken thighs and drumsticks – bone in, skin on. Slash them almost down to the bone to let the marinade sink in overnight or for a few hours, then let them cook off on the barbecue. Cook thighs and drumsticks, or a whole spatchcocked chicken.

Makes: enough for 4

---

8 free-range chicken thighs, or thighs and drumsticks,

or 1 free-range spatchcocked chicken

Season the chicken generously and, using a sharp chef's knife, make 2 or 3 slashes on each piece. Allow the chicken to marinate in your chosen marinade for a few hours in the fridge, or better still, overnight.

When the barbecue is ready, put the chicken on over a medium heat and cook thighs and drumsticks for 25–30 minutes and a whole spatchcocked chicken for 40–45 minutes, turning at least once. Baste with the marinade during the cooking process.

To check whether the chicken is cooked, insert a knife into the thickest part of the meat: the juices should run clear and the knife should feel scalding hot once you've removed it. I prefer to use a meat thermometer for accuracy, which should reach 70°C at the thickest part. Allow to rest for 5–10 minutes before serving.

STICKY JERK CHICKEN

This is proper festival chicken – a must for a summery barbecue. Definitely think about doubling up the quantities here, because people will come back for more.

Makes: enough for 4

8 free-range chicken thighs, or thighs
   and drumsticks,

or 1 free-range spatchcocked chicken

For the jerk paste

4 tbsp jerk seasoning (see page 52)

4 spring onions, roughly chopped

½ onion, roughly chopped

4 garlic cloves, peeled

5cm ginger, peeled

3 tbsp dark brown sugar

1 lime, juice only

2 heaped tsp sea salt flakes

1 Scotch bonnet chilli, deseeded

2 tbsp vegetable oil

Blitz the jerk seasoning, spring onions, onion, garlic, ginger, sugar, lime juice, salt, chilli and oil in a food processor or blender until you have a rough paste.

Using a sharp knife, slash the chicken thighs and drumsticks or spatchcocked chicken in a couple of places, almost down to the bone. Tip the chicken into a plastic bag or bowl along with the jerk paste and mix well, really working the marinade into the cuts. Tie up the bag, or cover the bowl, and transfer to the fridge to marinate for 2 hours to overnight.

See opposite for instructions for cooking chicken on a barbecue.

WORKS WELL WITH

Simple Sour Cream & Spring Onion Dip
   (see page 35)
Pickled Watermelon Rind (see page 126)
Pineapple, Chilli & Mint Salsa
   (see page 127)
Griddled Cos Lettuce with Blue Cheese,
   Lemon & Walnut Dressing
   (see pages 75 and 85)
Classic Coleslaw (see page 130)
Rainbow Potato Salad (see page 138)

TANDOORI CHICKEN

This is my favourite type of chicken, bar none. Note – much as it's the food of my childhood, this chicken won't be a lurid red, as that's usually food colouring – you'll get a more natural-looking reddish colour from the smoked paprika.

Makes: enough for 4

8 free-range chicken thighs, or thighs and drumsticks,

or 1 free-range spatchcocked chicken

For the marinade

6 tbsp natural yogurt

1 large lemon, zest and juice

5 garlic cloves, grated

5cm ginger, peeled and grated

2 heaped tsp ground cumin

1 tsp ground turmeric

2 heaped tsp smoked paprika

1 tsp mild chilli powder

A good grind of black pepper

1½ tsp sea salt flakes

To finish

2 tsp garam masala

2 tsp smoked paprika

Mix together the yogurt, lemon zest and juice, garlic, ginger and all the spices except the finishing ones.

Using a sharp knife, slash the chicken thighs and drumsticks or spatchcocked chicken in a couple of places, almost down to the bone. Tip the chicken into a plastic bag or bowl along with the marinade and mix well, really working the marinade into the cuts. Tie up the bag, or cover the bowl, and transfer to the fridge to marinate for 2 hours to overnight.

Just before you're ready to barbecue, sprinkle the top of each piece of chicken with a pinch of garam masala and smoked paprika. Turn to page 56 for instructions for cooking chicken on a barbecue.

WORKS WELL WITH

Freshly chopped coriander

Natural yogurt

Naan breads

Mango Salsa (see page 125)

   or Katchumber Salad (see page 124)

KOREAN BARBECUE MARINADE

Makes: enough for 4

8 free-range chicken thighs, or thighs and drumsticks,

or 1 free-range spatchcocked chicken

For the marinade

3 tbsp sesame oil

1 small bunch of spring onions, finely chopped

2 garlic cloves, crushed

10cm ginger, peeled and grated

2 tsp sugar

3 tbsp soy sauce

1 tbsp gochujang chilli paste

A splash of fish sauce

2 tbsp rice wine vinegar

100ml water

Sea salt flakes

WORKS WELL WITH

Quick Kimchi (see page 44)
Korean Summer Slaw (see page 132)
Pickled Watermelon Rind (see page 126)
Simple Sour Cream & Spring Onion Dip
(see page 35)

Heat a large frying pan. When it's hot, add the sesame oil, wait for small bubbles to form and then add the spring onions. Add a pinch of salt and sauté over a medium heat for 5–10 minutes, until the onions have softened and taken on a little colour.

Once the onions have browned, add the garlic and ginger and fry for another couple of minutes. Next add the sugar, soy sauce, chilli paste, fish sauce, vinegar and water. Bring to the boil, then reduce the heat and simmer for 5 minutes, until the sauce has thickened.

Taste and check the seasoning.

Using a sharp knife, slash the chicken thighs and drumsticks or spatchcocked chicken in a couple of places, almost down to the bone. Tip the chicken into a plastic bag or bowl along with the marinade and mix well, really working the marinade into the cuts. Tie up the bag, or cover the bowl, and transfer to the fridge to marinate for 2 hours to overnight.

Turn to page 56 for instructions for cooking chicken on a barbecue.

SMOKED PAPRIKA & LEMON CHICKEN

8 free-range chicken thighs, or thighs and drumsticks,

or 1 free-range spatchcocked chicken

For the marinade

1 tbsp smoked paprika, plus extra for sprinkling

1 lemon, zest and juice

4 sprigs of fresh rosemary, needles finely chopped

2 tbsp olive oil

1 tsp sea salt

Freshly ground black pepper

Mix the marinade ingredients together in a large bowl.

Using a sharp knife, slash the chicken thighs and drumsticks or spatchcocked chicken in a couple of places, almost down to the bone. Tip the chicken into a plastic bag or bowl along with the marinade, and mix well, really working the marinade into the cuts. Tie up the bag, or cover the bowl, and transfer to the fridge to marinate for 2 hours to overnight.

Just before you're ready to barbecue, sprinkle the top of each piece of chicken with a pinch of smoked paprika. Turn to page 56 for instructions for cooking chicken on a barbecue.

WORKS WELL WITH

Simple Sour Cream & Spring Onion Dip
   (see page 35)
Perfect Guacamole (see page 36)
Pink Pickled Onions (see page 42)

POLLO AL CARBON: ACHIOTE MARINADE

Pollo al carbón tastes exactly as it says on the tin: delicious, fiery, grilled chicken. As the saying goes, 'winner, winner . . .'

Makes: enough for 4

---

8 free-range chicken thighs, or thighs and drumsticks,

or 1 free-range spatchcocked chicken

For the marinade

1 tbsp coriander seeds

1 tbsp cumin seeds

½ tsp black peppercorns

2 cloves

2 tsp chipotle paste

1 tbsp dried oregano

2 garlic cloves, peeled

1 tsp fine salt

2 limes, juice only

6 tbsp vegetable or rapeseed oil

Using a pestle and mortar, crush the coriander seeds, cumin seeds, black peppercorns and cloves.

Tip into the small bowl of a food processor with all the remaining ingredients and blitz until a smooth paste is formed.

Using a sharp knife, slash the chicken thighs and drumsticks or spatchcocked chicken in a couple of places, almost down to the bone. Tip the chicken into a plastic bag or bowl along with the marinade and mix well, really working the marinade into the cuts. Tie up the bag, or cover the bowl, and transfer to the fridge to marinate for 2 hours to overnight.

Turn to page 56 for instructions for cooking chicken on a barbecue.

WORKS WELL WITH

Simple Sour Cream & Spring Onion Dip
  (see page 35)
Black Bean & Sweetcorn Salsa
  (see page 128)

WHOLE PORTOBELLO MUSHROOMS & ASPARAGUS

Barbecued mushrooms are a real winner – their texture combined with the smoky flavour of the barbecue is just lovely. Mushrooms are a great friend of garlic, so be generous with the basil, pine nut and garlic dressing.

Makes: enough for 4 as a side dish, or 2 as a main

4 large Portobello mushrooms, stalks trimmed

3 tbsp olive oil

250g asparagus, woody ends removed

Sea salt flakes

Light the barbecue.

Using a pastry brush, brush both sides of the mushrooms with olive oil and season generously. Drizzle olive oil evenly over the asparagus and sprinkle with a generous pinch of salt.

Allow the barbecue to come to a medium heat and place the mushrooms, top side down, on the grill along with the asparagus. Turn the asparagus over once or twice and cook until evenly charred.

Cook the mushrooms for 5 minutes, then flip them over and continue to cook for another 2–3 minutes. Again, cook until they have softened and are beginning to char.

Remove from the barbecue and serve immediately.

WORKS WELL WITH

Lemon, Dill & Feta Dressing (see page 83)
Basil, Pine Nut & Garlic Dressing
  (see page 84)

WHOLE AUBERGINE

Cooking aubergines whole is a brilliant way to ensure you have deliciously tasty, toasty, salty skin while keeping the centre of the aubergine tender.

Makes: enough for 4 as a side dish, or 2 as a main

2 aubergines

2–3 tbsp olive oil

Sea salt flakes

Light the barbecue and allow it to come to a medium heat: you are looking for it to be hot enough to cook the aubergines all the way through without totally burning the skins.

Using a pastry brush, lightly oil the aubergines and generously season the skins. Place the aubergines on the barbecue for 20–25 minutes, turning them every now and again, until evenly charred on the outside and cooked all the way through. To check for doneness, give the aubergines a squeeze: they should feel soft to touch.

Remove from the barbecue and allow to cool slightly. To serve, split the aubergines in half lengthways and sprinkle a teensy bit of salt on to the flesh.

WORKS WELL WITH

Lemon, Dill & Feta Dressing (see page 83)
Pink Peppercorn & Crumbled Goat's Cheese
    Dressing (see page 80)
Hot Satay Sauce (see page 33)

WHOLE CAULIFLOWER OR CAULIFLOWER STEAKS

The leaves of a cauliflower are equally delicious in their own right, so look out for particularly leafy ones – they're packed with nutrients and, simply drizzled with olive oil and cooked on the barbecue, make a delicious accompaniment to its whole counterpart.

Makes: enough for 8 as a side dish, or 4 as a main

1 large cauliflower, leaves removed

3–4 tbsp olive oil

1 tbsp nigella seeds

1 tbsp ground turmeric (optional)

Sea salt flakes

WORKS WELL WITH

Blue Cheese, Lemon & Walnut Dressing
(see page 85)
Chilli, Lime & Coriander Dressing
(see page 82)
Pink Peppercorn & Crumbled Goat's Cheese
Dressing (see page 80)

Light the barbecue.

Version 1: Trim the base of the cauliflower and make a small, cross-shaped cut in the base of the stalk.

Put the olive oil, nigella seeds, turmeric (if using) and a generous pinch of salt into a bowl and whisk to combine. Using a pastry brush, brush the marinade evenly over the cauliflower and set aside.

Allow the barbecue to come to a medium heat. Place the cauliflower on the grill, base side down, and cook for 40 minutes, turning once or twice during the cooking process. Try to minimise the amount of time you open the lid of the barbecue so that the cauliflower cooks all the way to the centre.

To check whether the cauliflower is done, insert a knife into the centre: it should slide in without resistance. If it still feels a little firm, move the cauliflower towards the outer edges of the grill and continue to cook for a further 10–15 minutes.

Once the cauliflower is cooked, remove from the heat and allow to cool slightly before serving.

Version 2: Without removing too much of the stalk, trim the woody base of the cauliflower. Using the whole width of the cauliflower, cut it into 1.5cm slices.

Put the olive oil, nigella seeds, turmeric (if using) and a generous pinch of salt into a bowl and whisk to combine. Using a pastry brush, brush the marinade evenly over the cauliflower and set aside.

Allow the barbecue to come to a medium heat. Place the cauliflower steaks on the grill and cook for 10 minutes, or until pleasingly charred. Flip the cauliflower steaks and cook for a further 5 minutes. The cauliflower should just yield to a knife inserted into the centre when it is cooked.

CORN ON THE COB & COS LETTUCE

The natural sweetness of corn on the cob benefits from a kick of smoke and heat on the barbecue. This dish works well either served straight away with plenty of butter, or made ahead and served as part of a big salad.

Makes: enough for 4 as a side dish, or 2 as a main

---

2 corn on the cob

2 cos lettuces, halved lengthways, roots kept intact

2–3 tbsp olive oil

Sea salt flakes

Freshly ground black pepper

Using a pastry brush, brush both the corn on the cob and the cos lettuces with oil and season generously.

Place the corn cobs on the barbecue over a high heat and cook for about 10 minutes, turning every now and again to ensure they cook evenly. Once the cobs are deliciously charred, remove from the heat.

Place the lettuces on the barbecue, cut side down, and cook for 3–4 minutes, until slightly charred. Flip, and cook for a further minute or so. Remove from the heat and allow to cool slightly before serving.

WORKS WELL WITH

Lemon, Dill & Feta Dressing (see page 83)
Blue Cheese, Lemon & Walnut Dressing
   (see page 85)
Chilli, Lime & Coriander Dressing
   (see page 82)

CHERRY TOMATOES, POINTY PEPPERS & HALLOUMI

Peppers and barbecues are a match made in heaven. They are just as delicious on their own as they are as an accompaniment to barbecued beef or lamb.

Makes: enough for 4 as a side dish, or 2 as a main

250g cherry tomatoes

2–3 tbsp olive oil

2 long pointy red peppers

250g halloumi, sliced

Sea salt flakes

Freshly ground black pepper

Lightly drizzle the cherry tomatoes with olive oil, sprinkle with a generous pinch of salt and wrap them neatly in a foil parcel.

Using a pastry brush, brush the red peppers and halloumi slices with olive oil and season well.

Place the vegetables and cheese on the barbecue over a medium heat. Cook the peppers until the skins have softened, turning every now again so that they cook evenly. You are looking for the peppers to be slightly charred without turning totally black. Check the cherry tomatoes after 10 minutes and remove from the heat once their skins have begun to split. The halloumi is done when golden brown and crisp.

Serve the peppers whole, or remove the stalks and slice into quarters lengthways. Remove the tomatoes from the foil and serve with the peppers and halloumi.

WORKS WELL WITH

Basil, Pine Nut & Garlic Dressing
  (see page 84)

LONG-STEM BROCCOLI

Thanks to the Maillard reaction, barbecued broccoli has a completely different flavour to steamed or boiled. It's the perfect accompaniment to fresh, crisp salads.

Makes: enough for 4 as a side dish, or 2 as a main

200g tenderstem broccoli, ends trimmed

1 tbsp olive oil

Sea salt flakes

Freshly ground black pepper

Drizzle the broccoli with olive oil and season generously. Place on the barbecue over a high heat and cook for 5 minutes, turning once, until lightly charred.

Serve immediately, with a generous helping of Vegan Summer Slaw (see page 129) and griddled pitta breads.

WORKS WITH

Pink Peppercorn & Crumbled Goat's Cheese
    Dressing (see page 80)
Blue Cheese, Lemon & Walnut Dressing
    (see page 85)
Steak (see pages 108–112)

PINK PEPPERCORN & CRUMBLED GOAT'S CHEESE DRESSING

Pink peppercorns, native to South America, are the ripe fruit of the Peruvian pepper tree. They have a sweet yet delicately peppery taste that complements the smooth, tangy goat's cheese. Lightly crushing the peppercorns is important in order to release their aroma and natural oils.

Makes: enough for 4

100ml olive oil, or 50ml olive oil
  + 50ml walnut oil

1 tsp pink peppercorns, crushed

1 tsp honey

1 tsp Dijon mustard

100g goat's cheese, crumbled

Sea salt flakes

Put the oil(s), peppercorns, honey and mustard into a bowl and whisk together until evenly combined. Stir through the crumbled goat's cheese. Season generously and taste to check that the flavours are well balanced. It should have a pleasing balance of sweetness, salt and acid.

WORKS WELL WITH

Long-stem Broccoli (see page 78)
Whole Aubergine (see page 69)
Cauliflower (see page 70)

CHILLI, LIME & CORIANDER DRESSING

This moreish and versatile dressing works well to balance the natural sweetness of some vegetables, such as corn on the cob. Adding a teaspoon of honey to the dressing will tip the balance of the scales in addictiveness.

Makes: enough for 4

---

1 lime, zest and juice

1 tsp light soy sauce

3 tbsp sesame oil

5cm ginger, peeled and roughly chopped

15g bunch coriander

1 bird's-eye chilli, deseeded

Place all the ingredients in a food processor and blend until you have a smooth sauce. If it looks too thick (you are looking for a sauce that will pour like single cream from a spoon) let it down with 1–2 tablespoons of water. Taste, and adjust the seasoning if necessary.

WORKS WITH

Whole Aubergine (see page 69)

Cauliflower (see page 70)

Corn on the Cob & Cos Lettuce
  (see page 74)

LEMON, DILL & FETA DRESSING

An easy, fresh way to finish off a plateful of roasted vegetables or indeed a salad.

Makes: enough for 4

½ lemon, zest and juice

150ml light olive oil

10g fresh dill, finely chopped

100g feta cheese, crumbled into small chunks

Sea salt flakes

Freshly ground black pepper

Put the lemon zest and juice, olive oil, dill and a generous pinch of salt and pepper into a bowl and whisk to combine. Add the crumbled feta and stir gently. Taste, and adjust the seasoning if required. Serve immediately, or keep covered in the fridge until needed – give the dressing a good shake before serving.

WORKS WELL WITH

Whole Aubergine (see page 69)

Cauliflower (see page 70)

Corn on the Cob & Cos Lettuce
(see page 74)

BASIL, PINE NUT & GARLIC DRESSING

Traditionally, pesto is made using a pestle and mortar. If, however, you don't have a heavy-duty pestle and mortar to hand, you can use a food processor, adding the ingredients in the same order.

Makes: enough for 4

50g pine nuts, toasted

½ garlic clove

15g fresh basil, leaves picked

100ml olive oil

Sea salt flakes

Freshly ground black pepper

Using a pestle and mortar, lightly crush the pine nuts until they begin to break down. Add the garlic to the mortar and crush again. Next, add the basil and half the olive oil, and continue to crush until the basil softens. You are looking for the leaves to break down and release their natural oils, but not quite so much that they begin to turn brown.

Transfer the contents of the mortar to a bowl and whisk in the rest of the oil, along with a generous pinch of salt and black pepper. Taste, and adjust the seasoning if needed.

WORKS WELL WITH

Long-stem Broccoli (see page 78)

Cherry Tomatoes, Pointy Peppers & Halloumi
    (see page 76)

Whole Portobello Mushrooms & Asparagus
    (see page 68)

BLUE CHEESE, LEMON & WALNUT DRESSING

I love this simple dressing – it's just as good with vegetables as it is with steak or barbecued chicken.

Makes: enough for 4

100g blue cheese, crumbled

½ lemon, juice only

100ml olive oil, or 50ml walnut oil
  + 50ml olive oil

50g walnuts, toasted and lightly crushed

Freshly ground black pepper

Put the blue cheese, lemon juice, oil(s) and a generous pinch of black pepper into a bowl and whisk to combine. Stir in the walnuts and taste to check that the flavours are well balanced – be mindful that the blue cheese is salty, so you may not need to add any additional salt.

WORKS WELL WITH

Whole Portobello Mushrooms & Asparagus
  (see page 68)
Cherry Tomatoes, Pointy Peppers
  & Halloumi (see page 76)
Adobo Sirloin steak (see page 109)
Long-stem Broccoli (see page 78)

SEA BREAM & SALSA VERDE

Super quick. Seriously tasty.

Makes: enough for 4

4 sea bream fillets, each weighing about 100g

For the salsa verde

8 anchovy fillets, chopped

1 small garlic clove, crushed

60g mixed fresh herbs, such as tarragon, mint and parsley, finely chopped

4 tsp Dijon mustard

2 tbsp capers, rinsed and finely chopped

5–6 tbsp olive oil

Sea salt flakes

Freshly ground black pepper

WORKS WELL WITH

Classic Tomato Panzanella (see page 142)
Classic Potato Salad (see page 139)
Vegetable skewers (see page 20)
Corn on the Cob & Cos Lettuce
   (see page 74)
Long-stem Broccoli (see page 78)

To make the salsa verde, combine the anchovies, garlic, herbs, mustard, capers, oil and a small pinch of salt and pepper and mix well. Taste first, before adjusting the salt and acidity: it may not need any extra seasoning because of the anchovies. If you're short of time, you could blitz the ingredients briefly in a food processor, then stir through the oil.

Tear two large squares of foil and lay one fish fillet, skin side down, in the middle of each square. Spoon 2 tablespoons of salsa verde on top of each of the fillets and top with a second fillet, this time with the skin facing towards you – like a fish sandwich.

Wrap the foil into a parcel – you'll need to be able to flip it over halfway without the filling leaking out. Place on the barbecue and cook for 15–20 minutes. The flesh should be opaque and just beginning to flake, and the fish should be warm all the way through.

GRILLED FISH TACOS

Synonymous with Mexico but with a twist of the northern hemisphere. The rich, intense flavour of mackerel comes into its own on the barbecue, especially when it's freshly caught. This is another recipe perfect for a barbecue on the beach.

Makes: enough for 4

---

2 tsp habanero or chipotle chilli paste

4 tbsp neutral-tasting oil

2 whole mackerel, cleaned and gutted, or 4 salmon fillets

Sea salt flakes

To serve

Pico de Gallo (see page 124)

Fresh coriander

4–6 tortillas, griddled

Fresh lime wedges

Combine the chilli paste, oil and a pinch of salt and mix well. Using a pastry brush, coat both the outside and the inside of the mackerel or salmon fillets with the mixture.

Place the fish on the prepared barbecue and cook for 10–15 minutes for mackerel, 10 minutes for salmon, flipping once halfway through cooking. Once cooked, the flesh should lift away from the bone and the eyes will be foggy. If you are unsure, insert a knife into the flesh for 10 seconds, then remove it: if it feels hot all the way along the knife, the fish is cooked.

Serve with some Pico de Gallo, a generous handful of fresh coriander leaves and a stack of warm griddled tortillas. Add lime wedges for squeezing over.

WORKS WELL WITH

Black Bean & Sweetcorn Salsa
   (see page 128)
Pickled Watermelon Rind (see page 126)
Simple Sour Cream & Spring Onion Dip
   (see page 35)
Perfect Guacamole (see page 36)

WHOLE RAINBOW TROUT

Rainbow trout has such a beautiful and delicate flavour that it's a shame to overshadow it with heavy spices. Nothing beats the flavour of freshly barbecued trout – on the bright white beaches of Mull if I can be choosy! – with a simple garlic mayonnaise.

Makes: enough for 4

---

1 fennel bulb, thinly sliced, using a mandolin

1 lemon, juice only

2 tbsp olive oil

2 whole rainbow trout, gutted and cleaned

Sea salt flakes

Freshly ground black pepper

Garlic Mayonnaise (see page 38)

Mix together the fennel, lemon juice and olive oil, and season with sea salt. Gently fill the inside of the trout with the fennel and wrap tightly in foil.

Cook on the barbecue for 15–20 minutes, until the fish is just cooked through. The flesh should lift away from the bone.

Serve the trout with a dollop of garlic mayonnaise, the warm fennel, and plenty of freshly ground black pepper. A hunk of fresh bread wouldn't go amiss.

WORKS WELL WITH

Classic Coleslaw (see page 130)

Herbed Potato Salad (see page 138)

Cherry Tomatoes, Pointy Peppers & Halloumi (see page 76)

Whole Portobello Mushrooms & Asparagus (see page 68)

SPICED SALMON FILLETS & BARBECUE SPELT CHAPATIS

So simple. So delicious. And a whole lot of fun to cook chapatis on the barbecue. Serve the salmon and chapatis with tzatziki and plenty of herbs. And some pickled watermelon rind if you've made some.

This is a great recipe for a barbecue on the beach. Marinate the salmon and make the chapatis ahead of time, using a smoking-hot frying pan, then assemble the rest of the ingredients with sandy hands when you get there.

Makes: enough for 4

2 tbsp ras el hanout

Chilli flakes (optional)

2 tbsp rapeseed oil

4 salmon fillets, or 1 side of salmon,
   trimmed and cut into 4 or 5 equal pieces

Sea salt flakes

For the chapatis

220g spelt flour, or 220g chapati flour

¼ tsp fine salt

2 tbsp rapeseed oil

100–150ml hot water

To serve

Coriander & Lime Tzatziki (see page 34)

Fresh herbs, such as dill, coriander
   and tarragon

WORKS WELL WITH

Whole Portobello Mushrooms & Asparagus
   (see page 68)
Pickled Watermelon Rind (see page 126)
Classic Potato Salad (see page 139)

Pop the ras el hanout, chilli flakes (if using) and oil into a bowl, along with a generous pinch of salt, and whisk together to form a smooth paste. Add the salmon fillets and set aside to marinate while you prepare the chapatis.

To make the chapatis, sift the flour into a bowl, add the salt and mix together. Make a well in the middle and add the oil, then pour in 100ml of hot water and mix together until a soft dough is formed. If the dough looks a little dry, add some more water; too wet, add a touch more flour. It should be soft and smooth. Knead the dough for 5 minutes.

Divide the dough into 8 balls and roll them out on a floured surface to about 16cm in diameter.

One at a time, or perhaps two, depending on the size of your barbecue, place the chapatis on the hot barbecue. Cook for 30–40 seconds, until the chapatis start to bubble, then flip and cook for a further 30–40 seconds. Squash any large bubbles with your spatula. Cover the chapatis with foil to keep warm while you cook the salmon.

Remove the salmon from the marinade and place on the barbecue. Cook for 4–5 minutes on each side, until just cooked through – the flesh should be just beginning to turn opaque.

Gently flake the salmon into large pieces. Sit them on top of a warm chapati, with a spoonful of coriander and lime tzatziki and a generous helping of fresh herbs.

BURGERS, STEAKS & SLOW COOKING

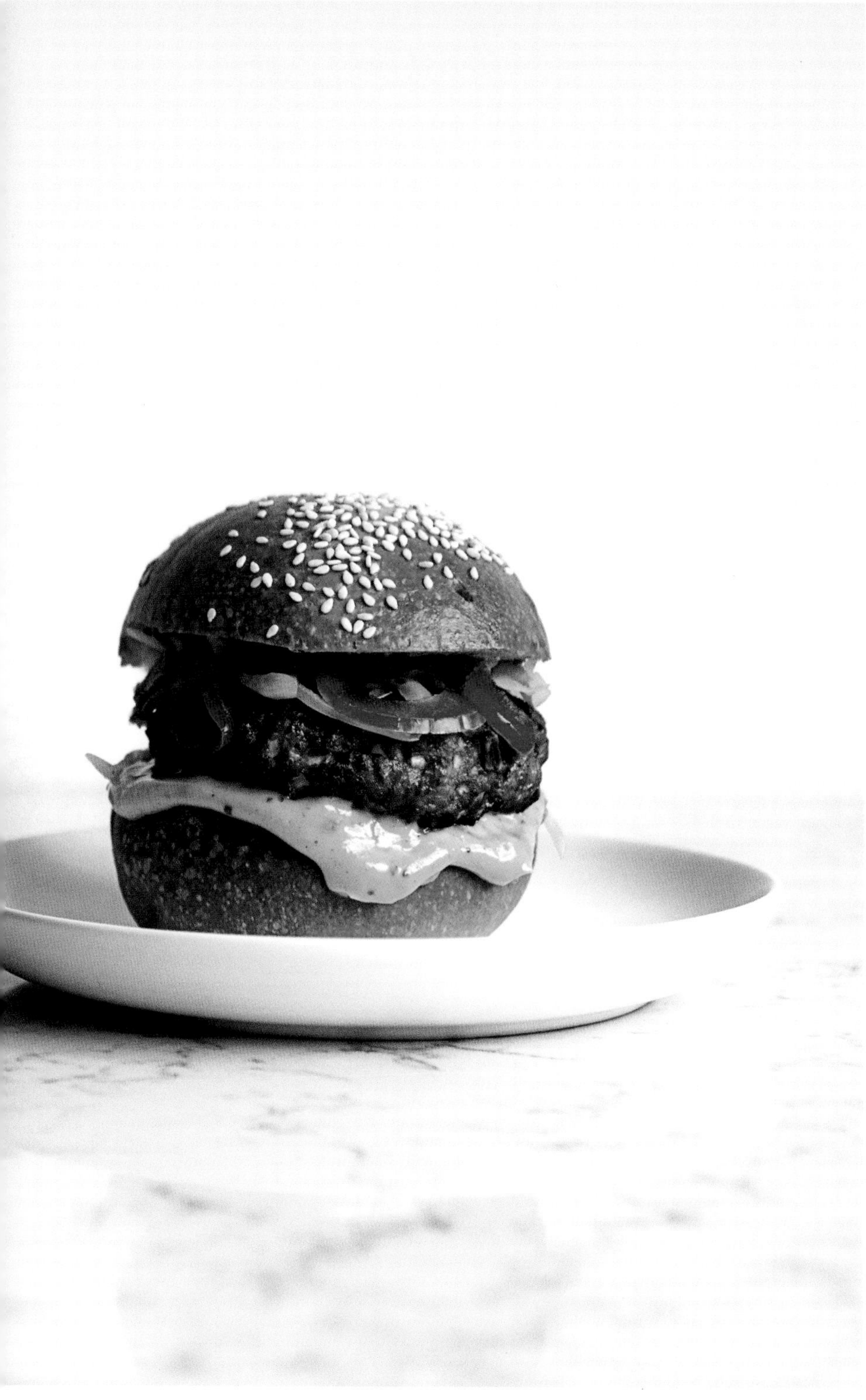

CLASSIC BEEF BURGERS

No messing about: the perfect homemade burger and how to cook it on the barbecue. If you can get hold of pinhead oatmeal I'd encourage you to use it, as it brings a welcome nuttiness and bite to the burger.

Makes: 6 patties

2–3 tbsp rapeseed oil

2 red onions, finely chopped

500g beef mince

4 anchovies, finely chopped

1 tbsp Worcestershire sauce

1 egg, lightly beaten

50g pinhead oatmeal or breadcrumbs

½ tsp salt

Freshly ground black pepper

25g Parmesan, grated

WORKS WELL WITH

Fennel, Courgette Ribbon & Orange Salad
  (see page 136)
Chipotle Mayonnaise (see page 38)

Heat 2 tablespoons of the rapeseed oil in a large frying pan, then add the onions and a pinch of salt. Cook over a medium-low heat for 10–15 minutes, until the onions have softened and browned. Remove from the heat and allow to cool.

When the onions are cool enough to handle, place in a bowl with the beef, anchovies, Worcestershire sauce, egg, oatmeal or breadcrumbs, salt and a generous pinch of black pepper. Mix together thoroughly with your hands, then cover and leave to stand for at least 1 hour.

Before cooking the burgers, break off a small piece, fry and taste to check the seasoning. Adjust if necessary.

Divide the mixture into 6 patties – each weighing about 105g. Return to the fridge until the barbecue is ready. With a pastry brush, lightly coat the burgers with oil.

Place on a hot barbecue and cook for 4–5 minutes on each side, until charred and hot all the way through – a thermometer inserted should read 70°C. Leave to rest for a few minutes before serving.

BEEF & HIDDEN MELTED CHEESE BURGERS

Blue cheese and beef are a classic combination, and in this burger, the hidden blue cheese centre flavours the meat from the inside as it cooks – a delicious and easy variation on the classic burger.

Makes: 6 patties

2–3 tbsp rapeseed oil

2 red onions, finely chopped

500g beef mince

4 anchovies, finely chopped

1 tbsp Worcestershire sauce

1 egg, lightly beaten

50g pinhead oatmeal or breadcrumbs

1/2 tsp salt

Freshly ground black pepper

60g blue cheese, such as Roquefort, divided into 10g cubes

Follow the instructions opposite until you have six patties. Flatten each patty into a disc, place a piece of blue cheese in the middle and close the mixture around it. Shape into a patty, taking care to ensure that the cheese remains in the centre of the burger.

Return the burgers to the fridge and chill until the barbecue is ready. Then lightly brush the burgers with oil.

Place on a hot barbecue and cook for 4–5 minutes on each side, until charred on the outside and wonderfully oozy in the middle – a thermometer inserted should read 70°C. Leave to rest for a few minutes before serving.

Remove from the heat and devour straight away.

WORKS WELL WITH

Herbed Potato Salad (see page 138)

Whole Portobello Mushrooms & Asparagus (see page 68)

Pickled Watermelon Rind (see page 125)

Mango Salsa (see page 126)

PORK, FENNEL & APPLE BURGER

Makes: 8 patties

2 tbsp rapeseed oil

1 fennel bulb, finely chopped

500g pork mince

½ tsp fennel seeds, toasted and crushed

1 star anise, toasted and crushed

1 tart apple, grated

1 egg, lightly beaten

50g pinhead oatmeal or 30g breadcrumbs

1 tsp fine sea salt

Freshly ground black pepper

Optional extra: fennel slaw

1 fennel bulb, thinly sliced

1 Granny Smith apple, thinly sliced

4 sprigs of fresh mint, chopped

4 sprigs of fresh fennel, leaves picked and roughly chopped

2 tbsp mayonnaise (see page 38)

1 lemon, juice only

Sea salt flakes

Freshly ground black pepper

WORKS WELL WITH

Pickled Watermelon Rind (see page 126)

Any whole veg (see pages 66–85)

Saffron Mayonnaise (see page 38)

Heat a large frying pan. Warm the oil, then add the fennel and a pinch of salt. Cook over a medium-low heat for 10–15 minutes, until the fennel has softened. Remove from the heat and allow to cool.

When the fennel is cool enough to handle, place in a bowl along with the pork mince, toasted spices, apple, egg, oatmeal or breadcrumbs, salt and a generous pinch of black pepper. Mix together thoroughly, using your hands, then cover and leave to stand for at least an hour to allow the flavours to develop.

Before cooking the burgers, break off a small piece, fry and taste to check the seasoning. Adjust if necessary.

Divide the mixture into 8 patties – each weighing about 105g – and return to the fridge until the barbecue is ready.

To make the fennel slaw, mix the ingredients together in a large bowl.

Using a pastry brush, lightly coat the burgers with oil. Place on the hot barbecue and cook for 10–12 minutes, turning once, until charred on the outside and warm all the way through – a thermometer inserted should read 71°C. Leave to rest for a few minutes before serving with the slaw.

SPICY LAMB KOFTE BURGERS

Barbecues and lamb are a winning combination. The natural sweetness of the lamb works so well with the smoky flavour of the barbecue. These koftes are excellent as part of a big spread, with warm flatbreads and mountains of fresh slaw. They are arguably even more delicious the next day.

Makes: 6 patties

½ tsp cumin seeds

½ tsp coriander seeds

½ tsp fennel seeds

500g lamb mince

1 garlic clove, crushed

2 tsp fine sea salt

½ tsp black peppercorns

½ tsp ground cinnamon

½ tsp chilli flakes

2–3 tbsp rapeseed oil

Heat a frying pan and toast the cumin, coriander and fennel seeds for a minute or so, until fragrant. Lightly crush using a pestle and mortar, then put into a large bowl along with the lamb mince, garlic, salt and the remaining spices. Leave to stand for at least an hour, to allow the flavours to develop.

Before cooking, break off a small piece, fry and taste to check the seasoning. Adjust if necessary. Shape the mince into 6 patties, each weighing about 105g. Using a pastry brush, lightly coat the outside of each kofte with oil.

Place the koftes on a hot barbecue and cook for 4–5 minutes on each side, until nicely charred and hot all the way through. Leave to rest for a few minutes before serving.

WORKS WELL WITH

Flatbreads
Coriander & Lime Tzatziki (see page 34)
Vegan Summer Slaw (see page 129)

SMOKY BLACK BEAN BURGERS

Makes: 4–6 patties

1 tsp cumin seeds, crushed

½ tsp ground cinnamon

2 tsp smoked paprika

1–2 tbsp rapeseed oil

16 spring onions, finely chopped

2 x 400g tins of black beans, rinsed, drained and dried using kitchen paper

2 garlic cloves, crushed

1 red chilli, finely chopped

2 tablespoons aquafaba (liquid drained from tinned chickpeas)

30g breadcrumbs

1 teaspoon fine sea salt

Freshly ground black pepper

1 lime

To serve

Pico de Gallo (see page 124)

Fresh herbs

WORKS WELL WITH

Corn on the Cob & Cos Lettuce
   (see page 74)
Chilli, Lime & Coriander Dressing
   (see page 82)
Pickled Watermelon Rind (see page 126)

Heat a frying pan. Toast the spices for a minute or so to release their fragrances.

Heat another frying pan, warm the oil and add the spring onions. Sauté for 8–10 minutes, until softened, then remove from the heat and allow to cool.

Place the black beans in a food processor and blitz briefly, until they begin to break down but without turning mushy. Put them into a bowl along with the toasted spices, spring onions, garlic, chilli, aquafaba, breadcrumbs, salt and a pinch of black pepper. Mix well until combined.

Shape the mixture into 4–6 patties, each weighing about 80g, and place in the fridge for at least 30 minutes to firm up.

Light the barbecue. Using a pastry brush, lightly coat each patty with oil. Cook on the barbecue for 5 minutes on each side, until nicely charred. Remove from the heat and serve immediately, with a generous squeeze of lime juice, some Pico de Gallo and plenty of fresh herbs.

Note: You can use the chickpeas you've drained to make Chickpea & Carrot Burgers or a quick hummus. Place 400g chickpeas, ½ garlic clove, juice of 1 lemon, 2 tablespoons of tahini, a generous pinch of sea salt, a twist of black pepper and 3 tablespoons of olive oil in a food processor. Pulse to combine, then season as required.

CHICKPEA & CARROT BURGERS

These are just as delicious hot as they are as leftovers the next day.
Thankfully this recipe makes enough to spare.

Makes: 8 patties

2–3 tbsp rapeseed or olive oil

4 shallots, finely chopped

1 x 400g tin of chickpeas, rinsed
and drained

2 carrots, grated

2 eggs, lightly beaten

2 tbsp harissa paste

1 tsp sea salt flakes

100g sourdough breadcrumbs

30g fresh coriander leaves, finely chopped

Fresh mint leaves (optional)

2 limes, juice only

Heat a large frying pan over a medium heat. Warm 2 tablespoons of the oil and add the shallots. Sauté for 15–20 minutes, stirring frequently, until softened and evenly browned. Remove from the heat and allow to cool.

Place the chickpeas in a food processor and blitz briefly, until they begin to break down but without turning mushy – it's nice to retain some texture. Decant them into a bowl along with the carrots, eggs, harissa paste, salt, breadcrumbs, herbs and shallots. Mix well until evenly combined.

Shape the mixture into 8 patties and put into the fridge, or freezer, for a couple of hours to firm up before cooking.

Brush each patty lightly with oil and cook for 5 minutes on each side – turning gently – until nicely charred. Remove from the heat and serve immediately, with the lime juice squeezed over.

WORKS WELL WITH

Flatbreads
Coriander & Lime Tzatziki (see page 34)
Vegan Summer Slaw (see page 129)

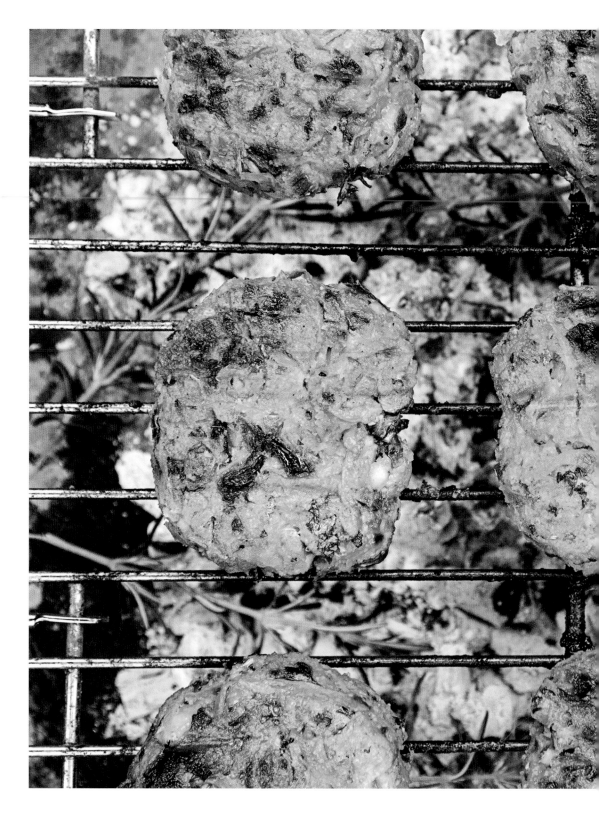

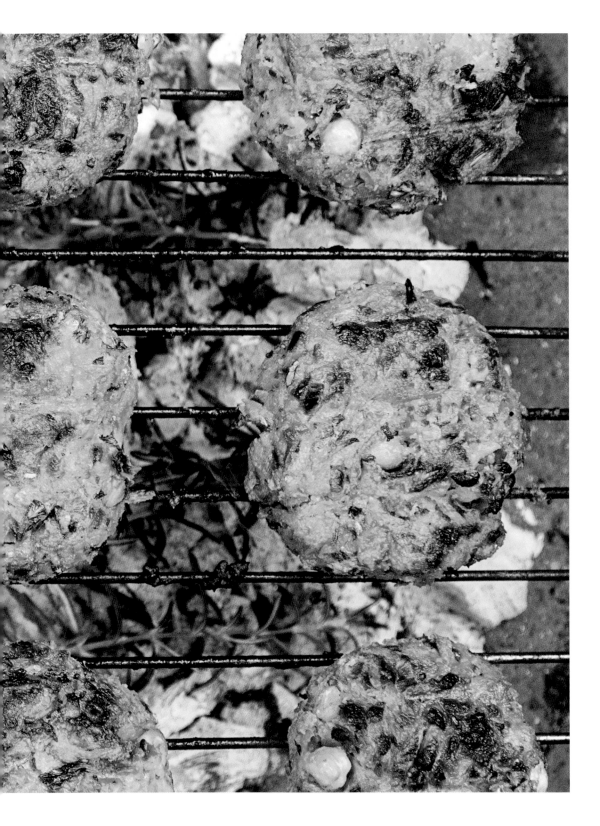

RIB-EYE STEAK

Rib-eye steak is a total winner on the barbecue. It's marbled with fat, which makes it flavourful and tender once cooked. Salting your steak well and in good time is so important to enhance the flavour of the meat.

Makes: enough for 2 people

2 rib-eye steaks, roughly 200g each

Your chosen marinade,
  see pages 112–115

To prepare the steak, trim away any wildly excess fat, and pop it on a plate covered in your chosen marinade. Cover and refrigerate until needed, allowing the beef to come back upto room temperature for 20–30 minutes before barbecuing.

Cook over a high heat for about 3–4 minutes on each side for medium rare; 4–5 minutes for medium; and 5 minutes for well done.

To check whether the steak is done to your liking, press it with your fingers: it will feel soft when rare or springy for medium-rare and firm when well done. Alternatively, check doneness by using a meat thermometer – 46°C rare, 51°C medium-rare, 57°C medium, 63°C medium-well done – the temperature will rise another couple of degrees while the steak is resting. Leave to rest for 5–10 minutes before serving, in order to allow the proteins to relax and the juices to distribute evenly throughout the meat.

WORKS WELL WITH

Chipotle Mayonnaise (see page 38)

Vegan Summer Slaw (see page 129)

Classic Potato Salad (see page 139)

Classic Tomato Panzanella (see page 142)

Cherry Tomatoes, Pointy Peppers & Halloumi
  (see page 76)

SIRLOIN, SKIRT OR BAVETTE STEAK

Sirloin, skirt or bavette steaks are all good quick-cook options for the barbecue. While sirloin is a classic choice, skirt and bavette are gaining in popularity. When well-marinated, cooked medium-rare then sliced thinly, they have a wonderful texture. The adobo marinade on page 112 is particularly good with skirt or bavette.

Makes: enough for 2 people

---

2 x 200g sirloin, skirt or bavette steaks

Your chosen marinade,
  see pages 112–115

Coat the beef in your chosen marinade, then cover and refrigerate until needed.

Allow the beef to come up to room temperature for up to 30 minutes before you want to barbecue.

Cook the steak over a high heat for 3–4 minutes per side for medium rare, and 4–5 minutes for medium – see opposite page for tips on checking the done-ness of the meat.

Take the steaks off the barbecue, and leave them to rest loosely covered in foil for 5–10 minutes before eating – this will make such a difference to the texture.

WORKS WELL WITH

Chipotle Mayonnaise (see page 38)

Vegan Summer Slaw (see page 129)

Classic Potato Salad (see page 139)

Classic Tomato Panzanella (see page 142)

Cherry Tomatoes, Pointy Peppers & Halloumi
  (see page 76)

ADOBO MARINADE

This Mexican-style marinade with fruity ancho chillies works perfectly with hanger, skirt or bavette steak. Perfect for steak tacos with salsa alongside.

Makes: enough for 2

2 x 200g skirt, hanger or bavette steaks

For the marinade

30g dried ancho chillies

1 garlic bulb

1 tsp ground cinnamon

1 tsp cumin seeds, crushed

5 cloves, crushed

½ tsp freshly ground black pepper

1 tsp dried oregano

2 tbsp apple cider vinegar

1 tsp fine salt

Place the chillies in a small bowl and cover with boiling water. Leave to rehydrate for 30 minutes to an hour.

Preheat the oven to 220°C/200°C Fan/Gas 7. Wrap the garlic bulb tightly in foil and place in the oven. Roast for 20 minutes, or until soft. Remove from the oven and allow to cool.

Take the steak out of the fridge and let it sit for 20 minutes to take the chill off.

Remove the chillies from the bowl, reserving the water, and remove the stalks and seeds. Place the chillies in a food processor along with the spices, oregano, vinegar, salt and 6 tablespoons of the chilli water.

Once the garlic is cool enough to handle, squeeze the soft flesh out of each clove and into the food processor. Blitz until a smooth paste is formed, adding more chilli water if necessary.

Coat the steak with the marinade and barbecue as per the instructions on page 109.

CLASSIC MUSTARD, WORCESTER & THYME

Makes: enough to marinate 2 steaks

2 x 200g rib-eye, sirloin or skirt steaks

For the marinade

1 tbsp Dijon mustard

3 tbsp Worcestershire sauce

6 tbsp olive oil

10g fresh thyme, leaves picked and finely chopped

1 tbsp cumin seeds, crushed

Sea salt flakes

Freshly ground black pepper

Combine all the ingredients in a bowl and whisk together. Add a generous pinch of salt and some freshly ground black pepper. Taste, and adjust the salt if necessary. Add the steak to the mixture and turn so it's well covered on both sides. Cover and refrigerate for 2–4 hours.

Take the steak out of the fridge and let it sit for 20 minutes to take the chill off before barbecuing as per the instructions on pages 108–109.

LEMON, GARLIC & ROSEMARY

Makes: enough to marinate 2 steaks

2 x 200g rib-eye, sirloin or skirt steaks

For the marinade

1 large garlic clove, very finely chopped

½ tbsp lemon juice

½ lemon, zest only

1 tbsp olive oil

½ tsp sea salt

Freshly ground black pepper

3 sprigs of fresh rosemary, needles finely chopped

Mix the marinade ingredients in a shallow bowl, then turn the steak in the mixture so it's well covered on both sides. Cover and refrigerate for 2–4 hours.

Take the steak out of the fridge and let it sit for 20 minutes to take the chill off before barbecuing as per the instructions on pages 108–109.

PORK PIBIL

Pibil is a slow-roasting pork dish originating from the Yucatán peninsula in Mexico. It is usually composed of achiote paste, habanero chillies and citrus, traditionally lime. If you have time, marinate the meat the day before cooking.

Cook the pork shoulder slowly on a low barbecue – it'll be perfect when the guests arrive. When it's ready, stuff it into soft tortillas with pink pickled onions and some deliciously addictive toasted chilli peanuts.

Makes: enough for 8–12

1.2kg pork shoulder

1 litre vegetable stock

For the marinade

1 tbsp coriander seeds

1 tbsp cumin seeds

Freshly ground black peppercorns

2 cloves

1 tbsp habanero chilli paste

1 tbsp dried oregano

2 tsp fine salt

3 garlic cloves, peeled

1 x 400g tin of chopped tomatoes

3 limes, juice only

3 oranges, juice only

For the chilli peanuts

50g unsalted peanuts, toasted and lightly crushed

1 tsp chilli flakes

Sea salt flakes

To serve

Pink Pickled Onions (see page 42)

Soft tortillas

WORKS WELL WITH

Pickled Watermelon Rind (see page 126)
Whole Portobello Mushrooms & Asparagus (see page 68)
Classic Coleslaw (see page 130)

Using a pestle and mortar, crush the coriander and cumin seeds, black peppercorns and cloves.

Place the spices in a food processor with the chilli paste, oregano, 1 teaspoon of salt, garlic, tomatoes, lime juice and orange juice. Blitz into a smooth paste.

Using a large chef's knife, make 3 or 4 deep slashes in the meat. Pour the marinade over the pork and rub in.

Version 1: Preheat the oven to 160°C/140°C Fan/Gas 3. Place the pork and its marinade in an ovenproof casserole dish, then pour in enough stock to just cover the meat and place a lid on the dish. Cook in the oven for 4 hours, or until the meat is soft and falling apart. Light the barbecue.

Remove the pork shoulder from the casserole dish and place the dish on the hob over a medium-high heat. Reduce the sauce until it thickens – enough to coat the back of a spoon. There should be a few centimetres of sauce left in the pan. Remove from the heat.

Meanwhile, place the pork on a hot barbecue for 10 minutes, turning it every now and again until all sides of the meat begin to char and caramelise. Remove from the barbecue. Using two forks, pull the pork into large chunks and return the meat to the casserole dish. Tumble the meat and sauce together until the meat is evenly coated.

Version 2: Light the barbecue. Place a baking sheet on the barbecue over an indirect heat. Remove the meat from the marinade and sit it on top of the baking sheet. Close the lid and cook for 4 hours, or until the meat is tender and falling apart. Remove from the barbecue.

Meanwhile, put the marinade in a saucepan, along with 500ml of stock. Bring to a gentle boil, then reduce the heat and simmer busily until the marinade has thickened and reduced by about two-thirds.

Using two forks, pull the pork into large chunks and return the meat to the casserole dish. Tumble the meat and sauce together until the meat is evenly coated.

For the chilli peanuts: tumble together the peanuts, chilli flakes and a generous pinch of sea salt.

Serve the pork with the pink pickled onions, a generous sprinkling of chilli peanuts and tortillas.

BARBECUE BRISKET

Beef brisket is brilliant for feeding a crowd. It's a low-cost cut with a punchy flavour, that you can leave on a low barbecue for hours; ready by the time your guests arrive and without having to pay it too much attention.

Makes: enough for 8, generously

750g beef brisket

1 tsp smoked paprika

1 tsp freshly ground black pepper

1 tsp cayenne pepper

1 x quantity of Classic Barbecue Marinade
(see page 49)

500ml beef stock

600ml lager

Fine salt

One day before cooking – or on the morning of cooking, if you are short of time – trim any excess fat and sinew from the beef and season liberally. Don't remove all the fat from the joint, however, as this is important for mingling flavours between the marinade and the meat.

To make the dry-rub, mix together the paprika, black pepper and cayenne pepper. Massage into the beef and set aside.

Next, whisk together the barbecue marinade and the beef stock.

WORKS WELL WITH

Korean Summer Slaw (see page 132)

Simple Sour Cream & Spring Onion Dip
(see page 35)

Classic Potato Salad (see page 139)

Mexican Chilli Peanut Sauce (see page 32)

Version 1: Preheat the oven to 160°C/140°C Fan/Gas 3.

Place the beef in a casserole dish and cover with the marinade and the lager. Cover the dish with a tight-fitting lid and cook in the oven for 4 hours, or until the meat is tender and falling apart. A knife inserted into the middle of the joint should slide in without any resistance.

Light the barbecue.

Remove the beef from the casserole dish and place the dish on the hob over a medium-high heat. Reduce the sauce until it thickens – enough to coat the back of a spoon. There should be a few centimetres of sauce left in the pan. Remove from the heat.

Meanwhile, place the beef on a hot barbecue for 10 minutes, turning every now and again until all sides of the meat begin to char and caramelise. Remove from the barbecue. Using two forks, pull the beef into large chunks and return the meat to the casserole dish. Tumble the meat and sauce together until the meat is evenly coated.

Version 2: Light the barbecue.

Place a baking sheet on the barbecue over an indirect heat. Sit the meat on top of the baking sheet, then close the lid and cook for 4 hours, or until the meat is tender and falling apart. You might like to baste the beef with the marinade every now and again, to prevent it from drying out.

Meanwhile, put the marinade and lager into a saucepan. Bring to a gentle boil, then reduce the heat and simmer busily until the marinade has thickened and reduced by about two-thirds.

Using two forks, pull the beef into large chunks and return the meat to the casserole dish. Tumble the meat and sauce together until the meat is evenly coated.

PINEAPPLE, CHILLI
& MINT SALSA

MANGO SALSA

CLASSIC PICO DE GALLO

CLASSIC PICO DE GALLO/KATCHUMBER SALAD

I love how this refreshing salsa, known as pico de gallo in Mexico and, with a slight variation, katchumber salad in India, works perfectly as a palate cleanser for strong flavours. The latter is a staple at my house with tandoori chicken and chicken curries.

Makes: 1 big bowl

400g cherry tomatoes, quartered

1 red onion, very finely chopped

1 red chilli, deseeded and very finely chopped

30g fresh coriander, finely chopped

1–2 limes, juice only

Sea salt flakes

And for katchumber salad

1 cucumber, cut into 5mm cubes

Mix the tomatoes, red onion, chilli and coriander together. If you're making katchumber salad, stir through the cucumber as well. Now add most of the lime juice and a big pinch of sea salt flakes, and taste – do you need more lime and salt? If yes, add them, taste, adjust and taste again until it's just right. Serve immediately.

Make ahead: Chop the tomatoes (and the cucumber, if using) and pop them into a sieve set over a bowl to drain away the excess juice. Keep the chopped chilli and coriander separate, and just before serving, stir everything together as above.

WORKS WELL WITH

Tandoori Chicken (see page 58)

Grilled Fish Tacos (see page 90)

Classic Beef Burgers (see page 98)

Spicy Lamb Kofte Burgers (see page 102)

MANGO SALSA

SALSAS

This colourful, refreshing salsa is perfect to serve with tandoori chicken. You can chop everything into little cubes, but it looks fantastic if you use a speed peeler to quickly turn it into a ribbon salad.

Makes: 1 big bowl

---

1 large firm mango, sliced

½ red onion, thinly sliced

1 red chilli, deseeded and finely chopped

1 lime, zest and juice

A handful of fresh mint/coriander,
   chopped

Mix everything in a large bowl just before serving, turning it gently with your hands to work the herbs, lime juice and chilli through the mango and onion.

Make ahead: Put the sliced mango in cold water in the fridge until ready to serve. Drain and stir through the prepared chilli, lime juice and chopped herbs just before serving.

WORKS WELL WITH

Any tandoori skewers (see page 28)

Sticky Hot Chipotle Ribs (see page 50)

Tandoori Chicken (see page 58)

Spicy Lamb Kofte Burgers (see page 102)

Smoky Black Bean Burgers (see page 104)

Grilled Fish Tacos (see page 90)

125 | SALSAS & SALADS

PICKLED WATERMELON RIND

This is a really simple and straightforward way to use up the watermelon rind that would otherwise be discarded. A jar of pickled rind will keep for up to a month in the fridge, and works as well with barbecued meat as it does with curries.

Makes: a 500ml Kilner jar

250ml white wine vinegar

250ml water

A pinch of chilli flakes

¼ tsp cumin seeds

100g caster sugar

1 tsp fine salt

1 bay leaf

Rind of ½ watermelon, peeled and diced into 5mm cubes

Put the vinegar, water, chilli flakes, cumin seeds, sugar and salt into a small saucepan, bring to a gentle boil, then reduce the heat and simmer for 2 minutes. Allow to cool completely.

Put the watermelon rind into a sterilised jar and pour over the pickling liquid. Keep in the fridge for up to a month.

WORKS WELL WITH

Pork Pibil (see page 116)
Jerk Ribs (see page 52)
Korean Barbecue Chicken (see page 61)

PINEAPPLE, CHILLI & MINT SALSA

This is such a refreshing salad – I love it on a hot summer's day. The sweetness is a perfect foil to barbecued meat – see below for serving suggestions.

Makes: 1 medium bowl

1 fresh ripe pineapple, peeled, cored
and cut into small chunks

1 small red onion, very finely chopped

1 red chilli, deseeded and finely chopped

15g fresh mint, finely chopped

1–2 limes, zest and juice

A pinch of sea salt flakes

Mix the pineapple, onion, chilli, mint and lime zest together, then add the lime juice and salt a little at the time, tasting as you go, until the flavours are nice and punchy. (You may need all or just one of the limes, depending on how juicy they are.)

Make ahead: If not serving immediately, keep the cut pineapple in the fridge in a large bowl, the chopped chilli and mint in a small bowl, and the red onion and lime juice in another small bowl. Mix it all together as above just before serving.

WORKS WELL WITH

Beef, chicken, pork, halloumi or paneer
    skewers with Rosemary, Cayenne
    & Brown Sugar Marinade
    (see pages 16, 22, 24 and 29)
Sticky Jerk Chicken (see page 57)
Pollo al Carbón (see page 64)
Grilled Fish Tacos (see page 90)
Sticky Hot Chipotle or Jerk Ribs
    (see pages 50 and 52)

BLACK BEAN & SWEETCORN SALSA

One for coriander lovers. It's nice to take the time to chargrill the sweetcorn, rather than just using the tinned stuff, as this adds depth to the salsa. Limes vary in their juiciness, so use your judgement.

Makes: enough for 6–8

2 corn on the cob

1 x 400g tin of black beans, rinsed and drained

½ watermelon, peeled and cut into 5mm dice

15g fresh coriander, leaves and stalks finely chopped

4 sprigs of fresh thyme, leaves picked

3–4 limes, juice only

1 red chilli, finely chopped

½ tsp ground cumin

4 spring onions, finely chopped

Sea salt flakes

Olive oil

WORKS WELL WITH

Pork Pibil (see page 116)
Grilled Fish Tacos (see page 90)
Spatchcocked Chicken (see page 56)

Place the corn on the cob on the barbecue over a high heat and cook for 10 minutes, turning every now and again, until evenly charred. Remove from the barbecue and allow to cool.

Alternatively, place a large frying pan over a high heat and chargrill the corn for 10 minutes, turning every now and again, until evenly charred. Remove from the heat and allow to cool.

In a bowl combine the beans, watermelon, herbs, lime juice, chilli, cumin and spring onions. Add a very generous pinch of salt and a drizzle of olive oil.

When the corn is cool enough to handle, use a chef's knife to shave off the kernels in clumps and set aside. When cool, add to the bowl.

Taste the salsa and adjust the seasoning and acidity if necessary. Both the sweetcorn and the watermelon are very sweet, so for the salsa to pack a punch, they need to be balanced with a generous quantity of lime juice and salt.

Toss the salsa together and serve immediately.

VEGAN SUMMER SLAW

I'm not exaggerating when I say this slaw goes with everything. The quantities in this recipe ensure enough to feed everyone generously, while leaving a little left over for you to enjoy again the next day. It's nice to take the time to prepare the vegetables by hand; if, however, time is in short supply, feel free to use the grating attachment on a food processor.

Makes: enough for 6, generously

150g blanched almonds

2 carrots, grated

½ red cabbage, shredded

1 fennel bulb, shredded, fronds reserved

3 lemons, juice only

3 tbsp olive oil

1 tbsp tahini

1 tsp Dijon mustard

A generous handful of mixed fresh herbs, such as mint, tarragon and dill, leaves picked and torn

Sea salt flakes

Freshly ground black pepper

WORKS WELL WITH

Smoky Black Bean Burgers (see page 104)
Chickpea & Carrot Burgers (see page 105)
Whole Portobello Mushrooms & Asparagus (see page 68)

Cover 100g of the almonds with water and leave to soak.

Place the carrots, red cabbage and fennel in a bowl, then add the lemon juice and mix well. Leave for 20 minutes, then strain.

Preheat the oven to 200°C/180°C Fan/Gas 6.

Roughly chop the remaining almonds and place in a small bowl with 2 tablespoons of water and a pinch of salt. Stir, then spread out on a lined baking tray and roast for 8 minutes, or until golden. Remove from the oven and set aside to cool.

Drain the soaked almonds and put into a high-speed food processor or blender with 200ml of cold water, the olive oil, tahini and mustard. Blitz until you have a smooth paste, similar to the consistency of mustard. Season generously with salt and pepper.

Pour the dressing over the vegetables and mix. Add the herbs and fennel fronds, then top with the toasted almonds and serve.

CLASSIC COLESLAW

This coleslaw is so good, I've been known to eat it by itself, or with a bit of cheddar on the side. A mix of mayonnaise and natural yogurt keeps the dressing light, as with the potato salad in this chapter.

Makes: more than you can believe

1 red onion

½ sweetheart cabbage

1 large carrot

For the dressing

40g mayonnaise

40g natural yogurt

1 tbsp extra virgin olive oil

1 tsp salt

1 heaped tsp Dijon mustard

Freshly ground black pepper

½ lemon, juice only

Very thinly slice the onion and cabbage, and cut the carrot into 5cm matchsticks.

Whisk all the dressing ingredients, then stir them through the coleslaw. Serve immediately. If making ahead, keep the vegetables in cold water and the dressing separately, and mix before serving.

WORKS WELL WITH

Any barbecued chicken or pork

HAIL CAESAR: THE ULTIMATE CAESAR SALAD WITH ROSEMARY CROUTONS

A Caesar salad is one of those recipes in which the flavour comes from the various types of salted ingredients rather than by just adding sea salt flakes. The anchovies and Parmesan each add layers of saltiness which are in turn balanced by the acidity of the lemon and mustard.

Makes: enough for 4, generously

2 sprigs of fresh rosemary, needles finely chopped

3 tbsp olive oil

200g sourdough, torn into bite-size chunks

2 romaine heart lettuces, leaves torn

2 chicory, larger leaves torn

10g fresh tarragon, leaves picked

Sea salt flakes

For the dressing

3 anchovy fillets

2 egg yolks

½ lemon, juice only

1 tsp Dijon mustard

1 garlic clove, crushed

75ml sunflower or rapeseed oil

15g Parmesan, grated, plus extra for shaving

Freshly ground black pepper

Preheat the oven to 220°C/200°C Fan/ Gas 7.

To make the croutons, mix together the rosemary, olive oil and a generous pinch of sea salt. Drizzle over the chunks of bread and mix well. Lay out on a lined baking tray and roast in oven for about 10 minutes, until golden. Remove from the oven and allow to cool.

Place the anchovies, egg yolks, lemon juice, mustard and garlic in the small bowl of a food processor and blitz until the mixture has increased in volume. With the blade still running, trickle the oil into the food processor slowly. Once all the oil is incorporated and the dressing has thickened, stir through the Parmesan and a pinch of black pepper.

Mix together the leaves, tarragon, croutons and dressing. Toss to combine, until the dressing is evenly incorporated. Top with Parmesan shavings and black pepper.

KOREAN SUMMER SLAW

This fresh, Asian-inspired slaw with sesame seeds and ginger is wonderfully light and refreshing – a million miles away from mayo-heavy supermarket offerings.

Makes: more than you can believe

8 spring onions, including the green bits

½ sweetheart cabbage, cut into quarters

2 medium carrots

For the dressing

1 tbsp sesame oil

2 tbsp white vinegar

1 tbsp soy sauce

5cm ginger, grated

1 garlic clove, peeled and grated

1 tbsp sesame seeds

Sea salt flakes

Cut the spring onions into 5cm segments, halve each of these lengthways, then thinly slice into long slivers. (Think about the way spring onions are cut when you order crispy duck with pancakes.) Dunk these into a bowl of cold water while you get on with very thinly slicing the cabbage and slicing the carrots into 5cm matchsticks. Put the cabbage and carrots into a bowl.

Mix the sesame oil, vinegar, soy sauce, ginger, garlic and sesame seeds together, along with a pinch of sea salt. Drain the spring onions, then add to the bowl and stir the dressing through the veg. Taste and adjust the salt, soy sauce and vinegar as needed, and serve immediately.

Make ahead: You can store the spring onions, carrot matchsticks and sliced cabbage in a big bowl of cold water in the fridge until it's time to make the salad – drain the veg really well in a colander, pat dry with a tea towel, then stir through the dressing as above.

WORKS WELL WITH

Korean Barbecue Chicken (see page 61)

Classic Beef or Beef & Hidden Melted
  Cheese Burgers (see pages 98 and 99)

Smoky Black Bean Burgers (see page 104)

Barbecue Brisket (see page 120)

WATERMELON, MINT, CUCUMBER & FETA SALAD

I don't think there's anything more refreshing than watermelon, mint, feta and cucumber – and I've served it in every possible combination, even on sticks as canapés. This version is much less structured, and incorporates my favourite smashed cucumber. Don't forget to save the watermelon rind for the pickle on page 126.

Makes: 1 really large bowl

1 cucumber

½ watermelon

200g feta cheese

20g fresh mint, roughly chopped

2 tbsp olive oil

1 lemon, juice only

Sea salt flakes

Freshly ground black pepper

Slice the cucumber into 5cm pieces, then pop them into a freezer bag and loosely seal. Lightly smash them with a rolling pin until you have variously sized chunks. Tip these into a colander along with a large pinch of sea salt, stir briefly, then set over a bowl – it'll help the cucumber pieces to lose water and firm up.

Meanwhile, cut your watermelon and feta into small wedges, no bigger than your largest pieces of smashed cucumber, and put them into a bowl with the mint. Mix the oil and lemon juice together. When the cucumber is ready, gently stir the dressing through everything. Taste, add a pinch of salt and pepper as needed, and serve immediately.

Make ahead: Keep your feta, smashed cucumber, sliced watermelon and dressing in separate bowls in the fridge and stir together with the mint just before serving.

WORKS WELL WITH

All Burgers (see pages 98–105)

Grilled Fish Tacos (see page 90)

Steak (see pages 108–112)

Smoked Paprika & Lemon Chicken
   (see page 62)

FENNEL, COURGETTE RIBBON & ORANGE SALAD

This salad is as pleasing in texture as it is in colour. It works beautifully with barbecued chicken or steak.

Makes: enough for 4, generously

2 courgettes

2 fennel bulbs, ends trimmed
and fronds reserved

1/2 lemon, juice only

15g fresh mint, leaves picked and torn

10g fresh dill, fronds picked

Seeds from 1/2 pomegranate (optional)

2–3 tbsp olive oil

A pinch of sea salt flakes

Freshly ground black pepper

Version 1

1 orange, zest and juice

Version 2
1 orange, peeled and segmented

WORKS WELL WITH

Steak (see pages 108–112)
Smoked Paprika & Lemon Chicken
(see page 62)
Pork Pibil (see page 116)
Corn on the Cob & Cos Lettuce
(see page 75)

Version 1: Using a vegetable peeler, peel the courgette down its length to create ribbons. Halve the fennel bulbs and slice down the faces, using a mandolin.

Place the courgettes and fennel in a bowl, add the lemon juice, herbs, orange zest and juice, pomegranate seeds (if using) and olive oil and season generously with salt and pepper. Tumble everything together gently, check the seasoning and serve immediately.

Version 2: Using a vegetable peeler, peel the courgette down its length to create ribbons. Halve the fennel bulbs and slice down the faces, using a mandolin.

Place the courgettes and fennel in a bowl, add the lemon juice, herbs, pomegranate seeds (if using), orange segments and olive oil and season generously with salt and pepper. Tumble everything together gently, check the seasoning and serve immediately.

HERBED OR RAINBOW POTATO SALAD

Once you have a template for a potato salad, you can do so many interesting things with it – either handfuls or fresh herbs, or a colourful mix of fresh vegetables. An oil-based dressing keeps the salad light, which makes this a nice variation on the classic with mayo opposite.

Makes: enough for 6, generously

750g waxy salad potatoes, halved if big (I like Anya)

2–3 tbsp extra virgin olive oil

15g fresh flat-leaf parsley, finely chopped

15g fresh mint leaves, finely chopped

1 tsp sea salt flakes

Freshly ground black pepper

And for rainbow potato salad

A handful of sugar snap peas, halved

8–10 radishes, thinly sliced

4 spring onions, hinly sliced

1 x 165g tin of sweetcorn, drained

WORKS WELL WITH

Steak (see pages 108–112)

All burgers (see pages 98–105)

All chicken (see pages 56–64)

All ribs (see pages 48–52)

Corn on the Cob & Cos Lettuce (see page 75)

Bring a large saucepan of salted water to the boil and cook the potatoes for 10–15 minutes until they're just cooked through. (Take one out, and smash it with a fork against a plate to check for doneness.)

Once the potatoes are done, drain them well, then return them to the pan and immediately stir through the olive oil, herbs and salt. Taste, adjust the seasoning if needed, and serve warm or at room temperature.

If you plan to make the rainbow salad, add the sugar snap peas to the potatoes for the last 2 minutes of cooking time. Drain well, then stir through the olive oil and herbs as above, along with the radishes, spring onions and sweetcorn.

CLASSIC POTATO SALAD

My go-to potato salad – with a mix of natural yogurt and mayonnaise in the dressing, this is a fresher version of the classic. Leave the potatoes unpeeled for more nutrients.

Makes: enough for 6, generously

750g waxy salad potatoes, halved if big (I like Anya)

1 tbsp extra virgin olive oil

40g mayonnaise

40g natural yogurt

1 tsp smooth Dijon mustard

½ tbsp lemon juice

A pinch of sea salt flakes

Freshly ground black pepper

Optional: pick from

2 nice free-range eggs

90g crispy cooked bacon lardons

A handful of crumbled blue cheese

Fresh herbs: flat-leaf parsley or chives

WORKS WELL WITH

Steak (see pages 108–112)

All burgers (see pages 98–105)

All ribs (see pages 48–52)

Smoked Paprika & Lemon Chicken
  (see page 62)

Bring a large saucepan of salted water to the boil and cook the potatoes for 10–15 minutes, until they're just cooked through. (Take one out and smash it with a fork against a plate to check for doneness.)

Once the potatoes are done, drain them well, then return them to the pan and stir through the olive oil. Mix the mayonnaise, yogurt, mustard, lemon juice, salt and pepper together, then gently stir this through your potatoes. Taste, adjust the seasoning if needed, and serve warm or at room temperature.

If you plan to put eggs into the salad, pop a couple of room-temperature free-range eggs in with the potatoes for the last 7 minutes of cooking time. Take them out, chill them in a bowl of cold water, then peel and cut into quarters before adding them to the salad.

If you're adding crumbled blue cheese, bacon or chopped herbs, stir these through once the potatoes and dressing have cooled slightly.

CLASSIC TOMATO PANZANELLA

It's important here to use the best, ripest tomatoes that you can find. And it's nice to use a mixture of varieties. If your bread is not quite stale, preheat the oven to 200°C/180°C Fan/Gas 6, tear the bread into small chunks and leave it to dry out in the oven for 20 minutes. Remove from the oven and allow to cool – the bread should crisp up as it cools. A traditional panzanella recipe usually calls for the skins of the peppers to be removed; however, I think they are delicious left on – and a good source of vitamin C.

Makes: enough for 4, generously

4 tbsp apple cider vinegar

1 tsp fine salt

½ red onion, thinly sliced

6 tbsp olive oil, plus a little for the peppers

2 red peppers, stalks removed, deseeded and quartered

450g mixed cherry or plum tomatoes, halved

200g stale rustic sourdough, torn into bite-size chunks

2 tbsp capers, rinsed

1 garlic clove, crushed

4 anchovies, finely chopped

10g fresh basil, leaves torn

10g fresh mint, leaves torn

Sea salt flakes

Freshly ground black pepper

Put 1 tablespoon of vinegar, 1 teaspoon of fine salt and 200ml of water into a small saucepan. Bring to a gentle boil, then remove from the heat and pour over the onion. Leave the onion to macerate while you prepare the remaining ingredients.

Put a frying pan over a high heat. Lightly oil and season the red peppers, then place them in the pan, skin side down. Cook until lightly charred and beginning to soften. Press the peppers firmly with the back of a spoon or spatula every now and again in order to encourage them to soften and flatten. Flip the peppers and continue to cook until lightly charred on the other side. Remove them from the pan and allow to cool.

Place the tomatoes in a colander set over a bowl to catch the juice. Sprinkle with a pinch of sea salt, give them a shuggle and leave for about 20 minutes.

After 20 minutes, squeeze the tomatoes to encourage them to release their juices and put them into a bowl along with the bread, capers and drained onions. Slice the cooked peppers and add them to the bowl too.

Add the garlic, the rest of the vinegar and the anchovies to the tomato juice and whisk in the olive oil. Check the seasoning – the anchovies should provide enough saltiness without needing to add any extra salt. Pour the dressing over the salad and leave to infuse for half an hour. Finally, stir through the herbs and serve.

WORKS WELL WITH

Steak (see pages 108–112)
Whole Aubergine (see page 69)
Cauliflower (see page 70)
Smoked Paprika & Lemon Chicken
  (see page 62)
Sea Bream (see page 88)

GRIDDLED MANGO WITH LIME & COCONUT

Barbecued mango is totally addictive. I would recommend making extra, as it is as delicious hot off the barbecue as it is for breakfast the next day (I'd recommend it with Greek yogurt and muesli).

Liquid coconut oil is available in most large supermarkets. But if you can't find it, just use the solid stuff and melt it gently before using.

Makes: enough for 4

---

2 ripe mangoes, cheeks sliced off

2 tbsp liquid coconut oil

2 limes, zest only

100g coconut flakes

Light the barbecue and allow it to come to a medium heat.

To prepare the mango, score the flesh first in one direction and then in the other, to create a hexagonal pattern.

Place the coconut oil and lime zest in a bowl and stir to combine.

Using a pastry brush, lightly coat the flesh of each mango cheek with the mixture. Place on the barbecue, flesh side down, and grill for 10 minutes, until the flesh is evenly charred and soft all the way to the middle.

Scatter each mango cheek with coconut flakes and the remaining coconut and lime oil. I like to eat it straight away with a teaspoon, using the skin as a bowl.

GRIDDLED NECTARINES, PLUMS & PEACHES WITH HAZELNUTS & ROSEMARY

Orchard fruit on the barbecue is a revelation, and a good way to use up a glut of slightly under-ripe or ripe fruit. Rosemary and hazelnuts add a wonderful flavour and texture.

Makes: enough for 4

2 peaches, halved and stones removed

2 nectarines, halved and stones removed

6 plums, halved and stones removed

2 tbsp olive oil

25g hazelnuts, skin on, toasted and lightly crushed

2 sprigs of fresh rosemary, needles finely chopped

Sea salt flakes

Light the barbecue and allow it to come to a medium heat.

Using a pastry brush, lightly coat the flesh of the peaches, nectarines and plums with olive oil. Place on a barbecue and grill for about 5 minutes, until the fruits' natural sugars begin to caramelise. You are looking for the fruit to become nicely charred at the edges and the flesh to feel soft to the touch.

Once cooked, remove the fruit from the heat, allow to cool slightly, then tumble together with the hazelnuts in a large bowl or platter. Finish with another drizzle with olive oil, a sprinkle of rosemary and a teeny pinch of sea salt – this helps to balance the natural sweetness of the fruit and enhance its flavours.

CHOCOLATE PB & J S'MORES

After experimenting with a lot of different combinations (no complaints there), I reckon this is pretty much the holy grail of s'mores. They're easy to pack up in foil at home, and take along with you to outdoor barbecues to cook.

Makes: enough for 4, with a few extras

12 rich tea biscuits

4 tbsp crunchy peanut butter

4 tbsp good-quality raspberry jam

12 marshmallows

50g milk or dark chocolate

S'mores can be cooked on the leftover embers of the barbecue. Prepare them before you start to cook your main course, and whack them on once you've eaten it.

Divide a sheet of foil into 6 strips, roughly 6–8cm wide.

To assemble the s'mores, lay out 6 of the biscuits on the foil: these will form the bottom of each sandwich. Spread 1 teaspoon of peanut butter on each biscuit, followed by 1 teaspoon of jam. Next, pop one or two marshmallows (I prefer two) on top, followed by one or two squares of chocolate. If you have time, it's fun to let everyone make their own. Finally, top each sandwich with another biscuit and wrap tightly in the foil.

Cook on the barbecue for about 5 minutes, until both the marshmallow and the chocolate has melted. Serve straight away.

GRIDDLED PINEAPPLE & WATERMELON WITH CHILLI-MINT SYRUP

This is a wonderful way to finish a barbecue – the sugar in the pineapple and watermelon caramelises beautifully, and works so well with the chilli and mint dressing.

Makes: enough for 8

8 bamboo or wooden skewers, soaked

1 pineapple, chopped into 2cm cubes

½ watermelon, chopped into 2cm cubes

2 tbsp dark brown sugar

100ml water

A pinch of chilli flakes

2 sprigs of fresh mint, leaves picked and chopped

Light the barbecue and allow it to come to a medium heat.

For each fruity skewer you will need 3 pieces of pineapple and 3 pieces of watermelon. Starting with a piece of pineapple and finishing with a piece of melon, thread alternating pieces of fruit on to each of the skewers.

To make the chilli-mint syrup, put the sugar, water and chilli flakes in a small saucepan. Bring to a gentle boil, then simmer for 2 minutes, or until all the sugar has dissolved. Remove from the heat and add the mint leaves.

Place the skewers on the barbecue and grill for 6–8 minutes, turning every now and again, until evenly charred. Remove from the heat, drizzle with the syrup and serve.

ROASTED STRAWBERRY & MARSHMALLOW SKEWERS WITH CHOCOLATE SAUCE

An easy crowd-pleaser. Cooking the strawberries and marshmallows over glowing coals elevates this from the sort of skewer you'd get with a chocolate fountain. Like the s'mores, these skewers can be cooked on the residual heat of the barbecue. Prepare them before you cook, and pop them on once you've eaten your main course.

Makes: enough for 4

---

4 bamboo or wooden skewers, soaked

200g strawberries, hulled and halved

12 marshmallows

100ml double cream

100g dark chocolate, broken into chunks

2 cardamom pods, seeds removed and crushed

1/2 lemon, zest only

For each skewer you will need 5 pieces of strawberry and 3 marshmallows. Starting with a strawberry, thread alternating pieces of marshmallow and strawberry on to each skewer.

Place the cream in a saucepan and bring to a gentle simmer – until you just see bubbles beginning to form at the edges. Remove from the heat and allow to cool slightly before pouring it over the chocolate. It is important that the cream is not too hot or the mixture may split. Stir gently until the two are evenly combined, then add the cardamom seeds and lemon zest and set aside.

Place the strawberry skewers on the barbecue, turning them as soon as the marshmallows begin to melt and crisp at the edges. Keep a close eye on them, as once the marshmallows start melting, they will do so very fast.

Drizzle the skewers with the chocolate sauce and serve immediately.

Watermelon, Mint, Cucumber
& Feta Salad (see page 134)

Spiced Salmon (see page 94)

Mango Salsa (see page 125)

Classic Pico de Gallo
(see page 124)

Simple Sour Cream & Spring
Onion Dip (see page 35)

Pineapple, Chilli & Mint Salsa
(see page 127)

Sirloin Steak (see page 109)

Tandoori Chicken
(see page 58)